# The Credit Ninja

&

Ex-Collection Agent reveals

Credit Secrets that

Collection agencies

and

Credit Bureaus

do not want you to know!

&

*Young's Publishing*

Author: Nathan Young

Editor & Graphics: Nay Young

Graphics & Book Design: Mark Bibby

Copyright © 2013 Author Nathan Young  All Rights Reserved

The Credit Ninja

# DEDICATION

*This book is dedicated to my wife who is my best friend & the love of my life. You are my one true love; you are my gift from the heavens above. I loved you from the moment I saw you and I will continue to love you all through eternity. Without you this book would not be possible.*

*I love you Nay.*

## *Disclaimer*

We are not attorneys nor we aren't licensed attorneys in any State of the United States of North America. Any of the information here is not intended to be legal advice; the information contained in this book is for informational purposes only. If you need legal advice regarding your credit you should obtain legal advice from a licensed attorney. The information in this book doesn't guarantee that you will increase your credit score as your score is based on many different factors and laws. This book is written with the sole intention of personal use and strictly educational it is not a guarantee of any results.

PEOPLE WHO WANT TO UTILISE THE INFORMATION LAID OUT IN THIS BOOK ARE ADVISED TO DO THEIR OWN INVESTIGATION WHEN IT COMES TO MAKING DECISIONS AND ALL INFORMATION WE HAVE PROVIDED SHOULD BE VERIFIED INDEPENDENTLY BY YOUR OWN HIGHLY QUALIFED PROFESSIONALS. THE INFORMATION IN THIS BOOK SHOULD BE CONSIDERED CAREFULLY AND EVALUATED BEFORE MAKING A DECISION, ON WHETHER TO RELY UPON IT. YOU COMPLETELY AGREE THAT WE ARE NOT RESPONSIBLE FOR YOUR FAILURE FROM YOU ACTING UPON THE INFORMATION LAID OUT IN THIS BOOK.

**COPYRIGHT © 2013 The Credit Ninja ALL RIGHTS RESERVED**

NO PART OF THIS BOOK MAY BE REPRODUCED, STORED IN A RETREIVAL SYSTEM OR TRANSMITTED IN ANY FORM OR BY ANY MEANS, ELECTRONIC, MECHANICAL, PHOTOCOPYING, RECORDING, SCANNING OR OTHERWISE WITHOUT PRIOR WRITTEN PERMISSION FROM THE AUTHOR.

# ~.~ TABLE OF CONTENTS ~.~

| | |
|---|---|
| Dedication……………………………………… | Page III |
| Disclaimer and Copyrights…………………… | Page IV |
| Acknowledgement ………………………….. | Page VI |
| Introduction ………………………………….. | Page 1 |
| What makes me a Credit Expert? ……………… | Page 2 |
| Chapter One …………………………………… | Page 3 |
| Chapter Two ………………………………….. | Page 9 |
| Chapter Three ………………………………….. | Page 14 |
| Chapter Four ………………………………….. | Page 16 |
| Chapter Five ………………………………….. | Page 21 |
| Chapter Six ………………………………….. | Page 27 |
| Chapter Seven …………………………………. | Page 32 |
| Chapter Eight ………………………………….. | Page 36 |
| Chapter Nine ………………………………….. | Page 44 |
| Chapter Ten ………………………………….. | Page 53 |
| Chapter Eleven ………………………………….. | Page 63 |
| Chapter Twelve ………………………………….. | Page 75 |
| Chapter Thirteen …………………………….. | Page 85 |
| Sample Letters ……………………………….. | Page 91 |
| Conclusion ……………………………………. | Page 118 |
| About the Book …………………………….. | Page 119 |

# ACKNOWLEDGMENTS

My gratitude and love to my loving wife, my strength and rock without her this book would not have been possible. I appreciate her love & company, long work hours, patience, all her help on drafting and editing this book. Huge appreciation to my partner and good friend Mark Bibby for your creative genius, knowledge and graphics design, for your amazing patience while we were working out the "bugs" on this amazing book, Thank You Mark. Want to also say Thank you to my Parents and Brothers who gave me encouragement and believed in me. We as a team look forward to helping all the supportive readers who are in need of a Credit Ninja self-help book that would assist you achieve a better credit report and score by utilizing the best kept Credit Ninja Secrets.

# Introduction

This Book is written to help educate people about their credit, credit scores and the laws that shape how our credit scores will affect our everyday lives. It is no secret that our credit scores control our lives. Credit scores can determine what kind of house we can purchase, what car we can drive, the car insurance rates, the interest on our credit cards and even potential employers.

Unless you are very financially stable, pay for everything in cash or you are younger than 18 years of age; the chances are you have had to fill out a credit application for a car purchase, home mortgage, credit card application, opening a bank account, motorcycle purchase, RV purchase, etc.

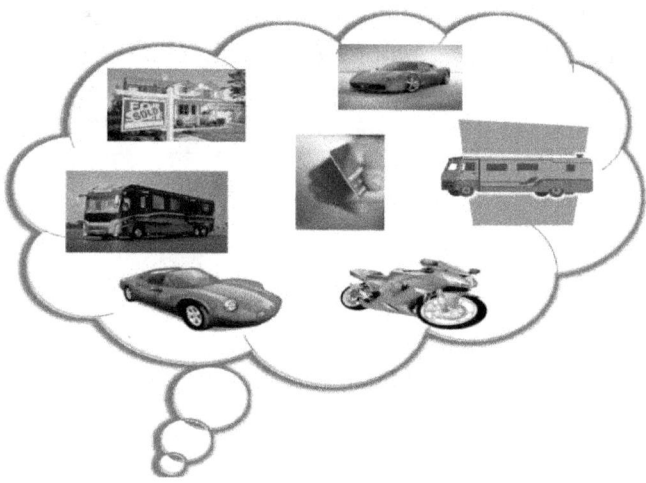

This book will help you understand your Credit Report, Credit Score and Credit Laws that everyone should know **but they do not want you to know**.

# What makes me a Credit expert?

You are probably asking yourself… What makes Nathan a credit expert?

Simply put I'm not an expert, but I have worked on the inside of a collections agency, I have spent several years studying and researching credit laws, credit repair and taught myself how to fix and repair my own credit.

## How I did that?

By using the same secret that has NEVER been revealed until now. In this book, **The Credit Ninja** there are **Secrets** that I am revealing to you on this book. The secrets are easy to use and it will help you understand your credit report and scores so that you can protect and also repair your own credit report. With these easy steps you can become a **Credit Ninja Warrior** and regain your life and credit back by avoiding all of the pitfalls of having a damaged credit record.

# Chapter 1

## CREDIT BASICS

In today's society your credit report and score affects your everyday life. Whenever you apply for a loan, a credit card or even apply for a job, chances are your credit report and score is pulled.

Depending on how you've managed your credit in the past can mean the difference of a credit approval or the dreaded credit denial. However no matter how careful we are with managing our credit and finances sometimes people experience an unforeseen hardship like loss of a job, an illness that can leave a person in financial bind. Sometimes bad things happen to good people it's just part of life and it's nothing to be ashamed of as this is one of those things in life that can be overcome with a little time and dedication to fixing and monitoring your credit report.

If you have ever applied for any type of credit whether it be a car, a job, a house, insurance of any type chances are you have a credit report and score, there is absolutely no way around it unless you have vanished off the map and if your reading this I'm guessing you have a few credit issues affecting your score or you are just trying to educate yourself so that way you can keep your good credit history or to help a friend or family member fix their credit reports.

While there is no guaranteed method on how to fix your credit score there are steps that you can take to fix errors on your credit report, which can ultimately increase your score from 50 to 100 points or more.

# Understanding Your Credit Report

## What is a credit score and how is it determined?

Your credit score is determined by several factors. The length of your credit history, your payment history, how many inquiries are on your report, along with your debt to income ratio. Don't worry I'll try to break it down so that it's easier to understand. Before I get into all of that we first need to understand what the different parts of a credit report are.

1. **Personal Information** - This section contains a record of your present and past addresses, your employment history and other personal information. Make sure they are correct.

2. **Credit Summary** - This section gives a history of all of your credit activity. Sometimes it may contain errors, be sure that the accounts mentioned in the summary are yours.

3. **Account Information** - This section gives you detailed information regarding your open and closed accounts which might contain accounts like your mortgage, credit cards, auto loans or leases and any other types of loans you might have.

4. **Negative Information** - This section will list any accounts that are in collections or that have had late payments of 30 days past due or more. This information must be closely monitored since fraudulent accounts can appear in this section.

5. **Inquiries** - This section lists all of the credit inquiries within the last two years. If you had your credit pulled in the last two years then the companies that requested a copy of your credit report will be listed here regardless of whether or not you were approved or denied.

6. **Credit Dispute Information** - This section has absolutely nothing to do with your credit score or personal information as it lists the contact information to the credit bureau so that you can dispute any information on your report that you believe to be incorrect.

*It is important to know the different parts of a credit report. If you don't know what these sections are and what information is in them, it would make it extremely hard for you to dispute any erroneous information in your credit report and hard to effectively raise your credit score.*

# Understanding Your Credit Score

Now that you understand the different parts of a credit report, let's look at some of the things that makes up your credit score.

1. **Length of Your Credit History** - Believe it or not the length of your credit history does in fact play a part in determining your credit score. This length is determined by the date you obtained a credit profile for most people this starts at 18 years of age and wanting to apply for their own credit card or loan.

Sometimes having no credit profile or a credit profile that has been opened for only a couple of months to two years can sometimes be better due to the fact that the person has no credit profile and are perceived by credit card companies and lenders to be a better credit risk than the person who has a long but poor credit history.

What do I mean by this? Well most lenders will assume a person who has little to no credit are less of a credit risk than the person who has a credit profile for a long time but has poor score on their credit reports. It all depends on the type of loan your applying for and how much along with the company's policies and procedures.

2. **Payment History** - If you have ever applied for credit and were approved for a loan your payment history can have a huge impact on your credit score. Regardless of how many open credit accounts you have if you've made all of your payments on time then chances are you are going to have a really good credit score. However if you have any collection accounts or were late on a loan payment could cause you to commit credit score suicide, as it will literally cause your score to plummet off the edge of a cliff at a very rapid pace.

But don't worry you can protect your score from hitting the pavement face first if you're willing to spend a little time and effort into repairing your damaged credit. It's easier to jump off a cliff than it is to climb back up so maintaining a good payment history it is vital to keeping a good credit score.

3. **Debt To Income Ratio** - Your debt to income ration also plays an important key role in determining your credit score. Your debt to income ratio is made up of two parts, which is all of your open debts and your yearly Income.

    A.) **All of Your Debts** - Your debt to income ratio is determined by all of your debts that are open and current along with any accounts that are in collections. Your debts are a total of all of this information, which can be found in your Account Information & Negative Credit sections of your credit report.

    B.) **Your Income** - This part is fairly self-explanatory as it is made up of your total salary before taxes are taken out regardless of how often you get paid, most companies where you are applying for the loan will go by your total yearly income.

## How is this used to determine how much credit you can obtain?

There is no real formula for this, because every creditor will use different information. For example some creditors will count your income, your debts, rent or mortgage payments and even your car payment; others will only use some of this information.

It would be nice if they all followed the exact same formula, as it would make it easier for us to determine whether or not we would be approved for a loan or credit way before you applied, which could save you some time, money and a needless credit inquiry that could have otherwise been avoided.

Now, let's go back to how companies use your debt to income ratio to determine your credit worthiness as they take the total of all of your debts and minus that from your total income and if you have any income left over it will increase your chances of getting an approval for whatever loan or line of credit you are applying for. This is how most companies will determine your debt to income ratio.

**Credit Inquiries** – You are probably wondering how credit inquiries can affect your credit score. Simply put whenever you apply for a credit card, loan, lease or insurance chances are the company you are applying with will pull your credit report, which will result in a credit inquiry. Most people believe that a credit inquiry doesn't affect their credit score and therefore they will continue to apply with several different companies until they find a company that will give them an extension of credit.

## What makes credit inquiries damaging?

Each inquiry can result in a drop of your credit score by 2, 3, 4 points per inquiry and if you have multiple inquiries chances are your score will drop from as little as 3 points to as much as a 100 points. Don't worry though as it is possible to remove a credit inquiry from your credit report, although it can be difficult to do sometimes it can still be done. If you're not able to remove any inquiries don't worry, an inquiry will only stay on your credit report for 2 years before it falls off your report.

# CHAPTER 2

## WHAT IS A CREDIT BUREAU & HOW TO OBTAIN A COPY OF YOUR CREDIT REPORT?

Now that you understand the different parts of your credit report and how your credit score is determined. Let's take a look at what a credit bureau is and how they affect you and your score.

### What exactly is a credit bureau?

There are three main credit bureaus Experian, TransUnion, and Equifax and you need to be familiar with all three of these because these are the repositories that store all of your personal and private information and they determine your credit score based on the criteria we discussed earlier.

Credit bureaus store all of the information that can be found on your credit report and sometimes they even store historical information like any of your past addresses and jobs that you might have had many years ago. Not all of this information is time barred.

I'll go into that a bit later on in this book for now lets keep it as simple as possible. Let's face it; all three of these credit bureaus play a major role in our daily everyday lives.

Whether you love it or hate it, credit bureaus will continue to manage our everyday lives as the information that these bureaus *have on our credit reports dictates what type of car we drive, what house we live in and even the types of jobs that will hire you.

Whenever you apply for a credit card or loan your credit report will be pulled from one or all of these credit bureaus, which will tell the person pulling your report whether you have good credit or a poor credit. If the company you are applying for credit with extends you a line of credit, chances are they will report your payment history on a monthly basis to one or all of these credit bureaus regardless of whether you pay your bills on time or not.

Either way the next person or company that pulls your credit will see this information and it will impact your score in either a positive or negative way which is why it's important to make your payments on time. If you're not applying for any type of loan but you're in the process of searching for a perfect job, chances are that potential employer will pull your credit report from one or all the three credit bureaus.

Now, I'm not sure why companies in the last 10 years decided to start pulling credit reports on potential employees; I've had known people in Human Resources office of some companies, they have told me that their company pulls credit reports to see how well that potential employee manages their finances. If the employee can handle their finances well, chances are they will be an employee that can handle their jobs well. I've had others tell me that if potential employee has bad credit they will be more likely to steal from the company. If you ask me I feel that is all wrong! Feels like just another way for a company to discriminate against potential employees.

Think about it, people fall into hard times especially in down economies like the one we recently went through or a person has had extremely high medical costs due to an illness or has recently gone through a divorce, regardless of why a person has bad credit.

Their poor credit rating doesn't make them less likely to steal or won't be able to manage their jobs properly, is usually the exact opposite. It's true that these kind of potential employees are more likely to show up on time and are willing to work extra hours and extra hard so that they can feed their families and get out of that tough financial spot.

Regardless of the potential employers reasons are for pulling your credit report, it's something you need to be aware of before you go on that big job hunt as you will gain multiple inquiries that will lower your score by a few points a piece. So the next time you go job hunting prepare yourself to know what type of job you want and make it a point to land the job the first time to avoid getting too many inquiries on your credit report.

## How to get a Copy of Your Credit Report?

There are several ways to get a copy of your credit report especially if you were denied credit within the last 60 days.

If you have applied for credit and were denied you will get a letter from the company who pulled your credit report that letter will outline the reasons why you were denied along with the address to the credit bureau that was used to pull your report, which will be one of the three credit bureaus that we discussed earlier. If you haven't been turned down for credit, but just want to see what is on your report, you are entitled to one free copy of your credit report from each one of the three credit bureaus.

You can do that by going to www.annualcreditreport.com from there you can enter your information and obtain a free copy of your credit report. Keep in mind that it will not contain your credit score on this free credit report.

If you want a copy of your credit score, you can obtain a copy from one or all of the credit bureaus by going to the credit bureau's website directly to obtain your score or you can use one of the services below to obtain your credit report. Regardless of how you obtain your credit report it's important that you obtain a credit monitoring, especially if you are planning on applying for **credit card** in the near future or planning to buy a **house** or a **car**.

Credit monitoring is a great way to make sure someone is not stealing your identity, which happens in today's society. Let's face it, we've all heard the horror stories and read the news articles of someone stealing the identity of another person and charging up huge bills for the victim to take care of later when they realize their identity has been stolen. By then it's usually too late and the damage has already been done.

Sometimes it can take years for the victim to regain their good credit history that is why it is important to continuously monitor your credit. That way when you do apply for that next big home or nice car, you won't feel like you've been run over with a semi-truck when you find out the hard way that you have been the victim of identity theft. Below are a few places that you can sign up for credit monitoring so that way you can keep this from happening to you.

**Lifelock** - This company will monitor your credit, provide you with a copy of your credit score and will provide you with up to $1,000,000 guarantee in the event that you become the victim of identity theft. (www.lifelock.com)

**IdentityForce** - This company will provide you with Identity theft protection, prevention services and worry-free identity theft solutions. They alert you when your personal data shows suspicious activity. (www.identityforce.com)

**Credit Karma** – This company goal is to empower consumers to more actively manage their credit and their financial health they also have interactive tools and simulators to help you learn how to anticipate changes in your credit score. (www.creditkarma.com)

**TrustedID** - This company has a great identity theft protection that monitors your credit, fraud alerts, spyware protection, and their black market internet scanning that scans the internet for unauthorized use of your information. They also have a $1,000,000 warranty that will protect you in the event you become a victim of identity theft. (www.trustedid.com)

# CHAPTER 3

## DISPUTING ERRORS ON YOUR CREDIT REPORT

Let's face it, no matter how perfect your credit report is, you still need to monitor your report. Sometimes there is incorrect information that can find its way into your credit report. Sometimes these small errors can cause a drastic drop in your credit score depending on what type of error it is.

Some of the common errors that can be found on credit reports are incorrect name spellings; typos in your address, the money amount on your open lines of credit, those can be reported incorrectly. It's also not unheard of to have late payment show up on your credit report when you actually made your payments on time. If that happens to you, it can cause a drop your score by 100 points or more.

Don't worry it's not the end of the world; sometimes credit information is reported longer than it should be reported or it's past the Statute Of Limitations. No matter what your reasons are for disputing incorrect information on your credit report it can be a vital part of the credit repair process as the information you are disputing will either get corrected or it will be removed from your credit report entirely which can ultimately help raise your credit score.

Whenever you dispute any information on your credit report the company you are filing your dispute with has 30 days from the date they receive the dispute letter to correct the information, remove it completely or give you a reason why the information is valid. By law they must respond within 30 days.

If they fail to respond within that time period the information must be removed from your credit report. This is true regardless if you are filing your dispute with the three major credit bureaus or if you are filing your dispute with a creditor or collector.

## How do you file a dispute?

There are several ways to file a dispute with the credit bureaus. You can file it online, all three credit bureaus have a form for submitting your dispute online. By mailing in your dispute in a letter via the United States Post Office or USPS. We recommend that you physically mail a letter rather than submitting your dispute online. One of the reasons is that it leaves a paper trail in the event that you ever have to sue or go to court if the credit bureau fails to respond to the dispute in the required 30 days.

Send your dispute via USPS and with return receipt requested, using the green 3x5 card on the letter so when they sign for the letter the card gets sent back to you as proof that they signed and received the letter. This is verifiable proof that the company won't be able to say they never received a letter from you.

# Chapter 4

## Credit Repair Companies
## Vs.
## Fixing Your Score Yourself

Now that you have the basics of how to dispute information on your credit report look at the two different ways you can fix and repair your credit score. Keep in mind that there is no true method to fixing your score regardless of whether you do it yourself or utilize the services of credit repair companies.

With that being said, making the decision to repair your blemished credit report is not only a difficult task but it's also a complicated one as it can be time consuming, expensive and it will often take up to a year or more for you to see any real results depending on what's type of information is on your credit report.

If you have a judgment it's not impossible to remove but it's definitely more difficult than trying to remove a late payment. The longer the account has been on your credit report the easier it is to remove.

### Now the question is …

*Do you utilize a credit repair company or Do you fix your credit score yourself?*

The answer for this one depends on each individual person as some people might enjoy taking on the challenge of fixing their credit reports themselves while others will want to take the easy road and use a credit repair company.

I know you have heard everyone say that there is no way to fix your credit score and that credit repair companies are all scams and a waste of money, which is far from the truth.

Utilizing a credit repair company can be extremely beneficial especially if you don't have the time, energy or patience and you have an extra $50.00 to $100.00 dollars a month for fixing your credit report. Then a credit repair agency is probably the best way to go. They are highly skilled and trained in credit laws and credit repair. If you utilize a credit repair company they will submit dispute letters to credit bureaus and collection agencies on your behalf.

It is very important to always check with the BBB to make sure the credit repair agency is a legitimate company since there are a lot of companies that claim great things, when in reality they don't. You will find a list of a few legitimate and well-known companies in the event you would rather utilize a credit repair agency. If you have good credit and you feel you don't have to ever fix your score yourself or utilize a credit repair agency, then you still need to make sure you monitor your credit reports.

Yes, it was mentioned earlier in this book but we can't stress enough how important that is to maintain a good clean credit profile. It's highly recommended that you use a credit repair agency if you don't have a lot of time on your hands because you have to carefully monitor the letters, follow up with disputes, keep a very detailed record of any and all contact with creditors and credit bureaus while you are disputing information. Is not recommended to try to fix your credit yourself unless you know you have the time to dedicate it. If you miss one letter or didn't record the times and dates of all letters and phone calls about your dispute, it can make it next to impossible to get that item corrected or removed from your credit report in the future.

This is not to scare you, it's a fact that you have to pay attention to detail when it comes to fixing your credit report as it could mean the difference between credit suicide or a zombie revival as you find your credit score slowly coming back to life.

Now, if you have the time and the patience to send out dispute letters, track all of the time and dates of all of your calls with the company that you are disputing the information with, then the best way to go is fixing your credit report yourself.

After all it is your credit report and chances are you will make sure that you record all communication correctly as you want to increase your score, taking those steps will help you qualify for that car or that dream house you've always wanted. You are your own best credit repair agency.

Let's take a look at some of the things that you can fix:

- **Collections**
- **Charged Off Accounts**
- **Judgments**
- **Bankruptcies**
- **Late Payments**
- **Erroneous Information**

All these can be removed or fixed regardless if you do it or utilize a credit repair agency. If you do choose to fix your own credit, I have included a chapter with dispute letters that I personally have used to increase my score by 150 points.

The letters included are $300.00 value if you use a credit repair agency. The cost of these letters would be even greater as you are basically paying a credit repair agency anywhere from $50.00 to $100.00 a month for them to send out similar letters for you.

Below I am providing you with links to some of the credit repair agencies that may interest you to use if you want to utilize a credit repair agency.

**The Credit People** - If you use this company they will give you a copy of your credit reports and scores. They even have 100% money back guarantee, which you can find out more about by visiting their site. (www.thecreditpeople.com)

**Lexington Law** - This company is extremely well known credit repair agency they will provide you with copies of your credit reports and they will handle the dispute process for you so spend time doing the things you love rather than spending your time disputing information on your report. (www.lexingtonlaw.com)

**The Credit Pros** - They will help you remove inaccurate information from your credit report. They also have a pay for delete business model. (www.thecreditpros.com)

**Credit Assistance Network** - If you are short on time or just don't want the hassles of writing letters and keeping track of all your disputes this company will handle it all for you. (www.creditagenda.com)

No matter how you choose to go about fixing your credit report keep in mind that your credit score is important to your everyday life also it's important to fix any errors on your report.

Remember that I can't guarantee you any type of results due to the complex nature of credit laws and credit repair.

# How about Debt Consolidation?

Sometimes life happens and we find ourselves in a financial bind. Whether it's a job loss, unexpected medical expense or some other reason that caused you to fall behind, that can happen to anyone. Sometimes the financial hardship can snowball and cause a person to fall behind on a majority or all of their bills almost overnight and it can cause you to think about applying for bankruptcy.

However, it doesn't matter how far a person is behind there are always ways to get out of debt or back on the road to getting past that financial roadblock without filing for bankruptcy. The fact is that bankruptcy is never a good idea as it can stay on a person's credit report for up to 10 years causing a credit score to drop to the bottom of the credit pool.

If you are considering bankruptcy, debt consolidation can be a really good alternative to bankruptcy. Some people have misconceptions about debt consolidation; debt consolidation can help you consolidate and settle your debts for less than the original amount owed making it a good alternative to bankruptcy. I would recommend anyone that is thinking about bankruptcy to consider debt consolidation before risking the damaging effects of bankruptcy.

Here are a few companies that I believe will help you avoid bankruptcy.

<u>CuraDebt</u> - This Company will help you settle your debts and help you avoid bankruptcy. (www.curadebt.com)

<u>National Debit Relief</u> - If you have credit card debt this company will help you settle your credit card debt for less than the original amount owed. (<u>www.nationaldebtrelief.com</u>)

# Chapter 5

## COLLECTION AGENCIES & YOU

Now that you know how your credit can affect your everyday life, it's time to learn what a collection agency is and how they can affect you and your credit.

## What is a collection agency?

A collection agency is a company that the past due or unpaid bills that you may have get sent to when the original creditor decides to sell your debt to the collection agency. Yes, I did say that creditors will sell your past due accounts to a collection agency, usually when they write off the debt.

The collection agency will buy the debt for pennies on the dollar, way less than what you owe. If the collection agency that originally bought your debt is unable to collect the debt then they turn around and sell it again. Sometimes the debt will get sold 4 or 5 times, sometimes even more before they all finally give up or the Statute of Limitations runs out.

I feel that the practice of debt buying should be illegal but it's not. Debt buying is an extremely huge business to the point that debt buying is a $143 billion dollar a year industry. With that comes a whole huge list of problems placing the practice of debt buying under a close eye by the Federal Trade Commission.

I'm sure by now you are wondering what kind of problems comes from debt buying if the FTC is scrutinizing the practice of debt buying. I will try to explain it for you without it getting too confusing. It can be a confusing subject but it's one you need to know especially if you have any account in collections.

Even if you don't, it is good for you to know in case you are ever in this situation. One of the biggest problems with the practice of debt buying is that most collection agencies don't follow State and Federal Laws when it comes to attempting to collect a debt.

Don't get me wrong as there are a few and I do mean a few collection agencies that actually will follow the laws, but for the most part they refuse to follow them because if they did follow State and Federal collection laws like the FDCPA or FCRA they would have a very hard time collecting any of the debts that they buy. I'll go into the FDCPA and FCRA laws a little further in another chapter.

I've have worked in collections company as a collector on debts that were 120 days past due or more. That is where I first became familiar with some of the laws that mandate the collection industry. I also have been in debtor's shoes, but hey! we all have made our share of stupid mistakes, it's how we learn from those mistakes that count. Now I'm married and pay all the bills on time. The point is I've been on both ends of the candle and learned a lot about credit laws.

***Disclaimer: I'm not expert and or a licensed attorney and this is strictly information that you can use anyway you see fit and is not any guarantee of any type of results.***

Since I've been on both ends of the candle, I've heard collectors tell debtors that they will get arrested if they don't pay their debts, I've heard collectors even threaten to sue debtors and garnish their wages if they don't pay and I've even heard them say that they will send someone to knock on your door to beat you up till you decide to pay them. I once had a collector leave me a message telling me they were calling in regards to a job application, as a collector they can't do because is against the law since is considered misrepresentation of a collection agency.

It is illegal for a collection agency to threaten a debtor with any of these harassing tactics regardless of whether the person actually owes the debt or not. The credit laws are in favor of the debtor rather than the collection agency which is good for you as you can use those laws as leverage to help clear your credit and ultimately raise your score.

## What Is The FDCPA?

The credit laws are always in favor the debtor more than it does the collection agency. The Fair Debt Collection Practices Act or FDCPA as it's known, is one of major acts that was put into place by the FTC and Federal government on September 20, 1977 to help protect consumers from abusive debt collection practices. I'll just cover some of the most important things that you need to know. Some of the things a collection agent CANNOT do when they are attempting to collect a debt are as follows:

1. They can't threaten you will jail time.

2. They can't call before 8:00am or after 9:00pm your time.

3. They can't threaten to sue you.

4. They can't call you at work if you have told them verbally or in writing that your employer doesn't allow calls at work.

5. They can't show up at your doorstep and if they do your local Police will gladly send someone to escort them off your property, don't hesitate to call a cop if they do.

6. They aren't allowed to call cell phone if you've given them a verbal notification to not call your cell phone again.

7. If you give collection agency a cease and desist notice they are no longer allowed to call you, the only way they can contact you are in writing by sending you a letter by mail only.

8. If they call a friend, family member or neighbor the Collector is not allowed to discuss any of your account information.

They cannot even say they are collecting on a debt; all they can ask if you know the person they are calling for and how to get a hold of the person. Remember that the collection agent are only allowed to call your friends and family **once**.

e.g. A collector calls your cousin two states away and your cousin talks to the collector, the collection agency is no longer allowed to call that person ever again regardless of whether or not your cousin knows how to get a hold of you or not.

I do need to elaborate on number 3 where I said a collection agency couldn't threaten to sue you in civil court. This is true they cannot verbally threaten you, but they can choose to file a civil suit against you in court and obtain a judgment in order to help them collect the debt if they feel that you will pay the debt if they take you to court. The collection agency just can't tell you they are going to take you to court in an attempt to collect a debt.

I always counter this one by telling the collector it's against the law to threaten with a civil lawsuit and they usually will back off and never call you again, but sometimes you get the idiot who just wants to argue this point with you. Don't waste your breath on ignorance just hang up, annotate the time and date of the call and send them a letter notifying them that are violating the FDCPA laws that were put into place to help protect you from this type of predatory collection practices.

The FDCPA will be your best weapon against predatory collection practices and it will help you remove items from your report along with the FCRA. While I didn't go into all aspects of FDCPA in this book. You can find a complete copy of the FDCPA on the Federal Trade Commission's website www.ftc.gov.

## What Is The FCRA?

Now that we have covered some of the ways that the FDCPA can help, now it's time to discuss what the FCRA is and how it can help you clear your credit. The Federal government in 1970 introduced the Fair Credit Reporting Act. The purpose of the Act was to help consumers protect their credit information and it was enacted to require banks to maintain certain records. Some of the things that the FCRA regulates are the type of credit information that is maintained on your credit report.

Here are some of the basic things that the FCRA covers.

1. It allows you to know what is in your credit file, allowing you to obtain copies of your credit report.

2. It allows you to one free copy of your credit report each year from the three major credit bureaus.

3. It allows you to verify the accuracy of your report especially for employment.

4. It allows you to dispute incorrect information on your credit report.

5. The FCRA also allows you to remove outdated, negative, information from your credit report that is 7 years or 10 years for a bankruptcy.

As you can tell the FDCPA and the FCRA are both powerful tools that you need to be familiar with especially when you are trying to remove inaccurate information from your credit report.

If you want to learn more about the FCRA you can find a copy of the FCRA on the Federal Trade Commission's website. (www.ftc.gov/os/statutes/031224fcra.pdf).

# CHAPTER 6

## STATUTE OF LIMITATIONS ON DEBT

Now that you're familiar with both the FDCPA and the FCRA is time to look at:

### What is Statute Of Limitations & Why does it concern me?

To answer this question is simple but fairly complex due to the fact that I have no idea what State you live in, I can only answer the basics. However because I don't know what State you live in I included a chapter that breaks down the Statute Of Limitations by State for your reference.

Now that we have that covered the Statute Of Limitations in most States keeps creditors and collectors from being allowed to sue you on any debt that is too old and outdated after a certain time period. Remember when I mentioned earlier on a previous chapter about time barred debts?

This is basically what I was talking about, this is the term that is used in the credit industry regarding debts that are past the SOL or Statute Of Limitations and they are time barred, meaning you can no longer be sued on that debt. The SOL on debt including in every State varies, but is usually anywhere from 3 to10 years depending on the type of debt and what State you live in.

## Importance Of Debt Validation

Now that you are familiar with some of the laws that will allow you to dispute incorrect or outdated information on your credit report, it's time to go into debt validation.

# What exactly is debt validation?

Debt validation is the process of disputing a debt that you believe is not yours or that you believe is past the Statute Of Limitations or that you know is yours but believe the collector doesn't have proper or enough information to prove that you actually owe the debt.

## Yes, I did say that!

You can validate any debt that you believe is not yours and you can also validate a debt that you know is yours but you think that the collection agency doesn't have enough documentation to prove in a court of law that is yours.

## If I know the debt is mine why would I validate it?

This is very simple; if you believe the debt is past the Statute Of Limitations sending the collector a simple debt validation letter will usually get them to cease any further collection activity against you. Keep in mind, sending those letters doesn't erase the debt; you still owe it to the original creditor. However, it could stop any further collection activities. This isn't' always the case as a creditor can still collect on the debt they just will no longer be able to sue you, which is exactly why most collection agencies will either sell the debt again or completely abandon it.

Remember when I mention that a collection agency will sell the debt for pennies on the dollar if they can't collect on the debt? and that some debts will be bought and sold more than once?

When you know this has happened to your debts, then it's a good time to send the collection agency that's harassing you a debt validation letter.

The reason why you would send a debt validation letter at this point is because that when debts are bought and sold it's all too often that the paperwork on your account is never transferred to the company who bought the debt as they usually do the debt buying electronically, only getting the basic information.

The information that the debt buyer gets is your name, address, place of employment, the type of debt, the original creditor and your social security number. Collection agencies that are debt buyers hardly ever get actual paperwork like, invoices, signed contracts, paid bills, canceled checks from previous payments or anything of that nature. The fact they don't get that information is in your favor.

**How is it possible that it can be in your favor when the collection agencies hardly ever get actual documentation regarding your accounts?**

Think about that for a moment ... Can your neighbor take you to court and sue you if one of your branches falls in their yard? Sure they can take you to court, unless your neighbor can document the time, date, the size of the branch, where it fell, the damage it caused along with documented proof that will prove without a doubt that the branch was yours rather than your neighbors. It could be extremely difficult to prove and the chances of your neighbor winning the lawsuit are probably zero.

I'm not saying they can't win; just their chances are just extremely slim. The same holds true for collection agencies, it's in your favor that they don't have documentation. If they try to take you to court sometimes the court will dismiss the case due to the collectors lack of documents and if you have filed a counter suit chances are you will win.

With that being said, it is extremely important for you to show up to court if a creditor takes you to court. It's all too often that a debtor won't show up to court because they think they won't win and take the judgment. Doing so can make it extremely difficult to obtain any type of credit for the next several years.

On that same token a lot of people do know that the creditor doesn't have proper documentation, they assume that it will be okay if they don't show up as they believe the judge will rule in their favor due to the lack of documentation.

That is far from the truth because even if the creditor or collector doesn't have documentation if you don't show up, a judge will always rule in favor of the collector for your failure to appear. This is called a default judgment and it means that you lost by default when 9 out of 10 times the judge would have ruled in your favor if you had shown up.

Meaning they can't prove that you own the debt without a shadow of a doubt which is why it's always important to show up. In the event you know you can't make it to your court date you must file a (**Motion To Continue Trial**). That motion for continuance is a document that explains the circumstances on why you can't make it to court and you would have this stamped and filed by the clerk of court.

Once this is filed with the court the judge will decide whether or not you have a valid reason to continue the trial. You need to give the court 10 to 20 days to make a decision, you need to file the motion on time and allow the judge enough time to make a decision on whether or not to allow you to continue trial.

If you file a **Motion To Continue Trial** make sure you send a clerk of the court stamped copy to the creditor or collection agencies attorney.

If you don't do so the other party will file a response saying that you didn't follow Rules of Civil Procedure and the court will most likely deny your request to continue trial. Because you need to send a copy of your Motion to the other party you must get 4 or 5 copies of your motion stamped by the clerk of courts.

Here's a list of the people that will need to have a copy of your motion depending on your courts Rules Of Civil Procedure your court clerk should be able to tell you who gets a copy keep in mind they are not allowed to give you legal advice.

1. For the Court Clerk

2. For Yourself

3. For the Other Party (Collector or Collection Agency)

4. For the Judge (You need the name of the judge)

All of the above people must have a stamped copy of your motion. This holds true regardless of what type of case you are filing a motion for.

Whenever you need to request a continuance or you are filing a response to a motion that was filed by a person in a case that you are a party. Motions are the documents that tell a court what you want done and how you want it done along with the reasons why the court should do it that way. I know, it doesn't seem fair, does it? I don't think so but it's the way our court system works.

# CHAPTER 7

## SIMPLE STEPS TO RAISE YOUR CREDIT SCORE

So by now you have the basic understanding of how to validate your debt. Now you wonder, What you can do to help raise your score while you are validating and disputing any incorrect information on your credit report?

There are wide ranges of simple steps you can do to help you raise your credit score all the way up to 100 or more points. If you use one or more of the things outlined below chances are you will slowly begin to see your credit score increase.

1. You can negotiate your past due debts to almost in half of the amount owed. Most of the time collectors will be willing to do this if they feel it's the only way they will be able to collect. Negotiate well and record the conversation because once they say **yes** you will have the verbal proof, also get the negotiation in writing and send them the letter with a self-addressed envelope to come to you, obtaining proof that they agreed to take half of the balance in writing.

2. Make your payments on time.

3. Negotiate lower interest rates once you begin to make payments on your high interest credit cards.

4. If you have a past due auto loan you can refinance it and get either a lower payment or interest rate, if not both.

5. You can also obtain a secured credit card that will help increase your score if you make the payments on time.

## Credit Cards and Personal Loans

Just like credit cards obtaining a credit card or personal loan can be beneficial to re-establishing a good payment history, which will ultimately increase your credit score. While this can be helpful to re-establishing your credit you have to be aware of some of the pitfalls that can go along with it if you are not careful on how much credit you obtain and management of payments can all play a vital role in the credit building process.

Obviously you don't want to obtain too much credit as this can sometimes lower your credit score and increase your debt to income ratio, especially if you go out and charge a bunch of stuff to your credit cards or borrow too much. Usually it takes **1** to **2** credit accounts to begin rebuilding your credit. It is very important that you need to make sure you make your payments on time, keep your credit card balances low and pay them off each month. Doing this keep your debt to income ratio low and will help increase your credit score. If you're applying for a personal loan you should always make a little more than your minimum payment. For example a loan car payment is $333.00 per month, pay about $350.00 or more per month. The extra amount goes towards the principal and helps pay faster the car loan.

This can work with any type of loan regardless of how much you borrowed. The good thing about this is that not only are you paying your loan faster but you are also rebuilding your credit while you're doing it. Are you wondering how to obtain a personal loan if you have less than perfect credit? Don't worry there are personal loans out there that are geared towards those with credit challenges. Sometimes banks will give you a secured loan no matter of your credit and credit history. Some banks will give you a loan that is secured by a savings account while others will give you a secured loan that is secured by CD.

e.g. When I was working on rebuilding my credit I opened a CD for $1,000. then I made a secured loan for $1,000 and a repayment term of 1 year. Doing this helped establish a good payment history. Not all banks have the same policies, check with your bank.

Below is a list of some companies that can offer you Credit Cards, Personal, Auto and Mortgage Loans to help you rebuild your credit and establish a good payment history:

## Credit Cards

Horizon Gold Card - This card will give $500.00 unsecured credit limit. It can only be used on Horizon's shopping network, it's a great way to rebuild your credit. They report to all 3 credit bureaus. (www.horizongoldcard.com)

CreditCards.com - This company has secured, and unsecured credit cards for those that need to begin rebuilding their credit by establishing a good payment history.

Net First Credit - This card will give $500.00 unsecured credit limit. It can only be used on Horizon's shopping network, it's a way to rebuild your credit. They report payments to all 3 credit bureaus. (www.netfirstplatinum.com)

MyCreditCardMatch - This company has a listing of over 100 credit cards so you are sure to find a secured or unsecured credit card that will help you gain that good payment history you need. (www.mycreditcardmatch.com)

## Personal Loans

CashNetUSA - This company will give you an installment loan regardless of your credit and will allow you to make payments. I've used this company in the past and I highly recommend them rather than doing a payday loan. (www.cashnetusa.com)

Prosper.com - This company is a peer-to-peer lending network where you can obtain a loan from other members who will help fund your loan. If you are looking for a loan to pay off a debt, start a business; Prosper is a great way to possibly fund a loan.

## Auto Loans

Carloan.com - This company will help you get a loan for a new or used car even if you have bad credit.

MyAutoLoan.com - This company will match you with up to 4 auto loan lenders based on your credit situation. For new or used auto loans as well as auto refinance loans.

RoadLoans.com - This company I've actually used myself in the past they have a high approval rate. They do cash back auto refinance loans as well as new and used auto loans.

Once you have removed or corrected errors on your credit reports and you have established a good payment history on all of your credit accounts you can begin the search for that dream home if you don't already own a home. If you do and you have a high interest rate or want to take out a refinance loan so that you can do those needed upgrades or to install that pool or Jacuzzi you've always been wanting. You don't have to have perfect credit to obtain a mortgage to buy a new home or to re-finance an existing one. You just need to be willing to go that extra mile to do the work towards your financial goals. There are all types of home purchase or mortgage refinance loans that will work with all types of credit situations.

## Mortgage Loans

TheEasyLoanSite.com - This company will match you with a lender that will help you obtain a loan based on your credit situation.

# Chapter 8

## UNDERSTANDING YOUR STATE'S STATUTES OF LIMITATION THAT EVERYONE SHOULD KNOW! BUT THEY DO NOT WANT YOU TO KNOW…

### What is Statute Of Limitations?

Statute of Limitations is the law that determines how long a person or entity can take you to court. When it comes to your debts the Statute of Limitations can be a good weapon that every good Credit Warrior should use to Ninja kick those pesky creditors and collection agencies in the face. Every State of The United States of America has their own Statute of Limitations on debt, ranging anywhere from 3 to 10 years depending on your State's laws.

**E.g.**: Let's say you have a debt with ABC Collections Company for an old wireless account for $400.00 and in the State you reside the Statute of Limitations for written contract is 5-years.

Now, because you live in a State with a 5-year Statute of Limitations, this means that the ABC Collections Company has only 5-years to take you to court for the $400.00 past due balance owed before the State's Statute of Limitations for written contract is up.

If ABC Collections Company does not take you to court in that 5-year period the State law is clear and per the Statute of Limitation it states that any Collections Company can no longer sue you for the $400.00 past due debt. What that means for You is that they cannot collect on this debt and no longer have any leverage to effectively collect on that account.

*I am sure you are smiling at this moment, this is a good Secret and the Collections Company Do Not Want You to Know this, so they can continue calling and trying to collect on this old debt that does not have any leverage.*

## Will The Statute Of Limitations Last Forever?

Let me talk to you about a couple of factors that are very important, if your debt is past the Statute of Limitations it is possible for the debt to **re-start** even if it is past your State's Statute of Limitations. Yes, I did say that, it could **re-start**!

Some people think it can't restart and this can cause you to commit credit suicide especially if the debt is several thousand dollars.

## How to avoid Re-Start?

I am sure you are asking yourself "How do I keep this from happening to me?" Simple, here are a few key guidelines that will help keep you from **re-starting** the Statute of Limitations on your debt.

1. Never admit that you owe the debt.
2. Never make a payment arrangement over the phone with the collector.
3. Don't make any payment even for a few pennies.
4. Always put any communication with a debt collector in writing.

Now, I know some of that sounds contradicting; you should always pay your debts, be a responsible consumer and make a written arrangement of payment to keep your debts off your credit report.

However, if you ever find yourself having any type of debt with a collection agency that it is **past** the SOL for your State, you should never admit to the debt or make any type of payment arrangement. If you do any of those things it will **re-start** your debt and open the floodgates allowing creditors and collectors to begin harassing you all over again.

What's worse, when this happens they can **re-start** the SOL on your debt and the collectors are more likely to sue you in court so that they can obtain a judgment and collect on the debt.

## Can a Debt Collector Still Call Me?

Most people think that just because their debt is out of the Statute of Limitations that a debt collector can no longer attempt to collect on the past due debt. This type of thinking is extremely dangerous to your credit health. Because if you begin thinking they can't, it could cause you to slip up and unknowingly **re-start** the SOL on your debt.

The debt collector can still attempt to collect on the debt, the only difference is they can no longer sue you or take you to court over it. If your debt is past the Statute of Limitations the chances of a collector being able to collect on the debt that you owe them is extremely low and they know it. Because of this, the chances of you actually getting further calls by a debt collector are extremely low especially if they know you are aware that the debt is past the Statute of Limitations.

Debt collectors hate it when you know about your State's Statute of Limitations, as it pretty much stops them cold from any further collection activity which is why knowing your State's Statute of Limitations can be a useful way to help you Ninja kick creditors and collectors in the face.

# When Does The Statute of Limitations Begin?

The answer to this question varies depending on the type of debt. In most States the Statute of Limitations begins when the consumer fails to make a payment for the first time on an account or when you get a call or letter from a debt collector for payment on the debt.

Whenever one of these two things happen is usually when the clock on the SOL begins to count down. Once the Statute of Limitations clock begins to countdown the creditor or collector only has that time period to sue you in a court in your jurisdiction. If the creditor or collector fails to bring legal action against you when the clock hits zero then it bans the creditor or collector from being able to sue you to collect the debt.

This is known as an Affirmative Defense that means you can turn around and counter sue the creditor or collector if they try to sue you after the Statute of Limitations runs out.

Here is a list of the type of debts that the Statute of Limitations on debt applies to:

1. **Open-Ended** - This type of debt usually pertains to credit cards or any other type of revolving account.

2. **Promissory Notes** - This type of debt is usually loans with fixed monthly scheduled payments like an auto loan or mortgage loan.

3. **Written Contract** - This is can apply to pretty much any type of loan like a personal loan, auto loan or payday loans.

4. **Oral Contract** - This is a verbal agreement between you and another person or entity whereby you verbally give a promise to repay a debt. This is how loans used to be done back in the day and they are extremely hard to prove in court.

## What Are The Different Types of Debt?

There are many different types of debt that you should be aware of such as secured debt, unsecured debt, and revolving debt.

All of these types of debt are important to know and understand as they do factor into when your State's Statute of Limitations will start and end for each type of debt.

**Secured Debt** - This type of debt is usually secured by another item or property sometimes this can be a house, car or other types of collateral. With secured debt the lender can seize the property and sell it to repay the loan if you were to ever default on a secured loan.

**Unsecured Debt** - With this type of debt the lender has no rights to seize property to collect on the debt. However if you do default on unsecured debt the lender can sell the debt to a debt collector or they can choose to take you to court so that they can collect the amount owed by garnishing your wages, intercepting your taxes or levying your bank accounts to **re-pay** the debt.

**Revolving Debt** - This type of debt is usually incurred from a credit card like a Visa, Master Card, American Express, Discover or store cards like JC Penney, Macy's, Wal-Mart, Sears or gas charge card.

**Take a look at the following table of the 50 States of United States Statutes of Limitations per types of Debt and type of contract, the numbers represent the years they can try to collect, sue or obtain judgment against you:**

| State | Written contract | Oral contract | Promissory notes | Open-ended accounts |
|---|---|---|---|---|
| Alaska | 3 years | 6 years | 3 years | 3 years |
| Arizona | 6 years | 3 years | 5 years | 3 years |
| Arkansas | 5 years | 3 years | 3 years | 5 years |
| California | 4 years | 2 years | 4 years | 4 years |
| Colorado | 6 years | 6 years | 6 years | 6 years |
| Connecticut | 6 years | 3 years | 6 years | 6 years |
| Delaware | 3 years | 3 years | 3 years | 3 years |
| District of Columbia | 3 years | 3 years | 3 years | 3 years |
| Florida | 5 years | 4 years | 5 years | 4 years |
| Georgia | 6 years | 4 years | 6 years | 4 years |
| Hawaii | 6 years | 6 years | 6 years | 6 years |
| Idaho | 5 years | 4 years | 5 years | 5 years |
| Illinois | 10 years | 5 years | 10 years | 5 years |
| Indiana | 10 years | 6 years | 10 years | 6 years |
| Iowa | 10 years | 5 years | 5 years | 10 years |
| Kansas | 3 years | 3 years | 3 years | 3 years |
| Kentucky | 15 years | 5 years | 15 years | 5 years |
| Louisiana | 3 years | 10 years | 10 years | 3 years |

| | | | | |
|---|---|---|---|---|
| Maine | 6 years | 6 years | 6 years | 6 years |
| Maryland | 3 years | 3 years | 6 years | 3 years |
| Massachusetts | 6 years | 6 years | 6 years | 6 years |
| Michigan | 6 years | 6 years | 6 years | 6 years |
| Minnesota | 6 years | 6 years | 6 years | 6 years |
| Mississippi | 3 years | 3 years | 3 years | 3 years |
| Missouri | 5 years | 5 years | 5 years | 5 years |
| Montana | 8 years | 5 years | 8 years | 8 years |
| Nebraska | 4 years | 4 years | 4 years | 4 years |
| Nevada | 4 years | 4 years | 4 years | 4 years |
| New Hampshire | 3 years | 3 years | 3 years | 3 years |
| New Jersey | 6 years | 6 years | 6 years | 6 years |
| New Mexico | 4 years | 4 years | 4 years | 4 years |
| New York | 6 years | 6 years | 6 years | 6 years |
| North Carolina | 3 years | 3 years | 5 years | 3 years |
| North Dakota | 6 years | 6 years | 6 years | 6 years |
| Ohio | 6 years | 6 years | 6 years | 6 years |
| Oklahoma | 5 years | 3 years | 5 years | 3 years |
| Oregon | 6 years | 6 years | 6 years | 6 years |
| Pennsylvania | 4 years | 4 years | 4 years | 4 years |

| | | | | |
|---|---|---|---|---|
| Rhode Island | 10 years | 10 years | 10 years | 10 years |
| South Carolina | 10 years | 10 years | 3 years | 3 years |
| South Dakota | 6 years | 3 years | 6 years | 6 years |
| Tennessee | 6 years | 6 years | 6 years | 6 years |
| Texas | 4 years | 4 years | 4 years | 4 years |
| Utah | 6 years | 4 years | 6 years | 4 years |
| Vermont | 5 years | 3 years | 6 years | 3 years |
| Virginia | 6 years | 6 years | 5 years | 6 years |
| Washington | 6 years | 3 years | 6 years | 6 years |
| West Virginia | 10 years | 10 years | 10 years | 10 years |
| Wisconsin | 6 years | 6 years | 10 years | 6 years |
| Wyoming | 10 years | 8 years | 10 years | 8 years |

**A bit more about the Laws…**

In the State of Georgia the Court of Appeals ended with a decision on January 24, 2008 case of *Hill v. American Express* that in the State of Georgia the SOL on a credit card is six years after the amount becomes due and payable. As you can tell that the SOL varies by the type of debt and along with the type of contract that was used when you originally agreed to the type of debt that was incurred. Knowing the Statute of Limitations will help you protect yourself from being sued in a court and will put an end to abusive debt collection practices by allowing you to finally strike back and Ninja Kick your debt collectors in the face.

# Chapter 9

## HOW TO SUE A DEBT COLLECTOR

If you have any debt in collections you may find yourself being a victim of a wide range of abusive debt collection practices. Debt collectors often use abusive bullying scare tactics that violate the FDCPA laws in an attempt to force you into paying your debts. The **_FDCPA_** allows you to sue a debt collector if they violate any of the laws and or provisions of the **FDCPA**. Here is a list that you can utilize to sue an abusive debt collector if they do or the following happens during an attempt to collect.

1. Calls before 8:00am in your time zone.
2. Calls after 9:00pm in your time zone.
3. Threaten you with legal action.
4. Threaten to send you to jail.
5. Calls you at work after you told them not to.
6. Threatens you with harm.
7. They call more than twice in a day.
8. Violates your Privacy Rights.
9. Call after you give them a Cease & Desist.
10. They refuse to validate your debt.
11. Fails to tell you they are a debt collector.
12. Reports false credit information to the Credit Bureaus.

If a debt collector does any one of the actions mentioned above, you have the right to take them to court and sue for damages of up to $1,000.00 plus you may get an award for your attorney's fees.

You may also be able to remove the collection item from your credit report permanently. It is always very important to document any and all of the communication that you have with a creditor or debt collector by making a note of the time, date and nature of the call regardless of whether the communication is by phone, fax, email, or regular mail.

Always write down who you spoke with and notes or a brief synopsis of the conversation. The rule of thumb is to answer the Who, What, When, Where and Why and document everything.

In case a debt collector attempts to sue you or they violate the **FDCPA**, this information will become a powerful weapon to Ninja Kicking the collector in the face! It will make it a lot easier for you to win a case against a debt collector. Just make sure you file your case against a debt collector, as the Federal Statute of Limitations on filing a lawsuit against a Debt Collector is **1 year**.

## How Do I File a Lawsuit Against a Debt Collector?

It is easy to file a lawsuit against a debt collector. The laws will vary by State but the procedures are similar. However you need to file the lawsuit with your State court or the Federal court. Keep in mind that the task of filing a lawsuit against a debt Collector can be confusing and challenging, especially if you are considering filing it without an attorney. You can file a lawsuit by yourself, but I would not recommend it, there are a lot of Legal rules and laws to consider when it comes to suing a debt collector.

Some of the things you need to do in order to file a lawsuit against a debt collector is you need the **burden of proof evidence** which is why you need to document everything. Also you need to obtain the proper forms from your State's Court and file the paperwork with the Court Clerk. Court may have fees when you want to file the lawsuit, check with your State's court what are the fees for filing a lawsuit. You will also need to follow Rules of Civil Procedure that require you to serve the company or person you are suing with a copy of the lawsuit that was filed with the court.

If you fail to properly serve the other party it could cause you to lose your case so you need to make sure you follow the Rules of Civil Procedure for the court you are filing the lawsuit in regardless if it is your State Court or Federal Court.

You can serve the other party and be in compliance with the Rules of Civil Procedure by utilizing one of the following ways to serve the other party.

1. Hire a Process Server to serve a copy of the lawsuit.
2. Have a Sheriff serve the other party.
3. Notice of Publication.
4. Send notice by USPS Mail Certified Return Receipt.

You can use any of these methods mentioned above to serve the other party. However, using a Notice of Publication will only be allowed if you have used all other options for serving the other party. The most common practice the courts will use a Sheriff to serve the other party.

If your court doesn't do that, you can hire a Process Server that is licensed by the courts for which they serve. You can find a list of Process Servers online or you can get a listing from the State court in which you live.

Most courts will charge a filing fee for your lawsuit against a debt collector. However, you can always ask for an award of any fees that you paid to file your lawsuit. You can also ask the court waive filing fees if you fall under a certain low income or on any type of government assistance. Every court varies when it comes to the income limits that are allowed when it comes to being able to file your lawsuit without fees. The court clerk will be able to tell you what limits are set for your State. Don't let the lack of funds scare you into not filing suit as sometimes it's the only way to put a stop on abusive debt collector and possibly get your debt removed.

## Courts by States

| State | Trial Courts |
|---|---|
| Alabama | Judicial Circuit, District, Small Claims Courts |
| Alaska | Superior, District, Small Claims Courts |
| Arizona | Superior, Justice of the Peace, Municipal Courts, Small Claims Courts |
| Arkansas | Circuit, District, City, Small Claims Courts |
| California | Superior, Small Claims Courts |
| Colorado | District, County, Small Claims Courts |
| Connecticut | Superior Court, Small Claims |

| | |
|---|---|
| Delaware | Superior Court, Court of Chancery, Court of Common Pleas, Justice of the Peace Court |
| District of Columbia | Superior, Small Claims Courts |
| Florida | Circuit Court, County Court, Small Claims |
| Georgia | Superior Court, State Court, Magistrate Court, Municipal Court |
| Hawaii | Circuit Court, District Court, Small Claims Court |
| Idaho | District Court, Magistrate's Division (small claims) |
| Illinois | Circuit Court, Small Claims Court |
| Indiana | Superior Court, City and Town Court, County Court, Small Claims Court of Marion County |
| Iowa | District Court |
| Kansas | District Court |
| Kentucky | Circuit Court, District Court |
| Louisiana | District Court, Justice of the Peace Court, |
| Maine | District Court, Superior Court |
| Maryland | Circuit Court, District Court, Small Claims |

| | |
|---|---|
| Massachusetts | District Court Department, Boston Municipal Court Department, |
| Michigan | Circuit Court, District Court |
| Minnesota | District Court, Conciliation Division (Small Claims) |
| Mississippi | Circuit Courts, Chancery Courts, County Courts, Justice Courts |
| Missouri | Circuit Court |
| Montana | District Court; City Court, |
| Nebraska | District Court, County Court |
| Nevada | District Court, Municipal Court |
| New Hampshire | Superior Court, District Court |
| New Jersey | Superior Court, Small Claims Section |
| New Mexico | District Court, Magistrate Court, |
| New York | District Court, City Court, Civil Court of the City of New York |
| North Carolina | Superior Court, District Court |
| North Dakota | District Court, Municipal Court |
| Ohio | County Court, Municipal Courts |
| Oklahoma | District Courts, Small Claims Courts |
| Oregon | Circuit Court, Justice Courts |

| | |
|---|---|
| Pennsylvania | Philadelphia Municipal Court, Magisterial District Judge |
| Rhode Island | Superior Court, District Court |
| South Carolina | Circuit Court, Magistrate Court |
| South Dakota | Circuit Court, Magistrate Court |
| Tennessee | Circuit Court, General Session Court |
| Texas | District Courts, Municipal Courts |
| Utah | District Court, Justice Court |
| Vermont | Superior Court |
| Virginia | Circuit Court, District Court |
| Washington | Superior Court, District Court |
| West Virginia | Circuit Court, Magistrate Court |
| Wisconsin | Circuit Court, Municipal Court |
| Wyoming | District Court, Circuit Court |

You can contact the court for your jurisdiction as you will be able to find the contact information for your state and county along with guides that will help you learn how to file your case with the court.

If you are filing your case by yourself rather than hiring an attorney to file your case; keep in mind it is not an easy task to do alone, it can be done but I would highly recommend that you seek the advice of a Licensed Attorney.

## Sample of a Complaint Form:

```
 1  Your Name
 2  Address
    City, State, Zip
 3  Telephone Number
 4
 5              IN THE UNITED STATES DISTRICT COURT
                FOR THE DISTRICT OF (Your Residential State)
 6
 7  Your Name,                )   CASE NUMBER WILL BE ASSIGNED
                              )   AT TIME OF FILING
 8         Plaintiff,         )
                              )
 9  vs.                       )
10                            )   COMPLAINT
                              )
11         Defendant.         )
12  _____      )
13
14
15                         **Jurisdiction**
                         (Separate Paragraph)
16
17
18                          **Complaint**
                         (Separate Paragraph(s))
19
20
21         COMPLAINT MUST COMPLY WITH (*Your State*) RULE
           (Search for your State Rule on How to submit a complaint)
22
23                           **Demand**
                         (Separate Paragraph)
24
25  Dated:_____
                                  (YOUR SIGNATURE IN INK)
26                                Your name typed or printed
27                                Address
                                  Telephone Number
28
```

## Collection Agency Communication Log

To keep track of all the communication you receive from a collection agency. Always keep extra copies of a log similar to the one below in your desk or any place in your home where you sit to annotate all the details of the conversation. Also after you fill this log place it in a folder with copies of the letters received from and sent to that collection agency in specific.

| Collection Agency Name | | Collector's Address | |
| --- | --- | --- | --- |
| Agent's Name | | Agent's Phone | ( ) |
| Debt they are collecting | | Original Creditor | |

| Date: | Time: | Type of action:<br><br>LR: Letter received<br><br>LS: Letter Sent<br><br>PCR: Phone Call received<br><br>PCM: Phone Call Made | Notes of the phone conversation. If it was a certified letter you sent, write the certified # |
| --- | --- | --- | --- |

____  _____  _____

____  _____  _____

____  _____  _____

____  _____  _____

# Chapter 10

# HOW TO KNOCK OUT A DEBT COLLECTOR

*In this Chapter you will find Simple Methods To Ninja Kick a Collector That It Will Knock Them Out…*

Dealing with a debt collector can be stressful, frustrating, tiring, and extremely annoying. Especially since a debt collector will harass you with annoying phone calls, they will sometimes use abusive language, send you letters, call your workplace, threaten you with lawsuits and sometimes even bodily harm which is why you need to know the simple methods to giving a debt collector a swift Ninja roundhouse kick that will knock them.

When a debt collector becomes abusive its normal to become frustrated, angry and it will stressed you out so much to the point where you may want to give in to the debt collector just to get them to go away. That's exactly why a debt collector will use these abusive and illegal debt collection practices as they know that most of the times you will give in and pay the bill even though it might be outside the Statute of Limitations, no proof of the debt or even worse they get beaten down enough to the point of paying a debt collector even if the debt isn't theirs.

If you end up giving into paying an abusive debt collector it is a sure fire way to commit credit suicide as it will **restart** the Statute of Limitations and if the debt isn't yours and you pay it you're taking responsibility for it, which means it now can legally be put on your credit report as a late payment.

**Never ever give into an abusive debt collector, as a majority of the time the debt collector has no real proof of the debt that means if the collections agency have no papers or proof to prove that the debt is yours in a court of law then you are not responsible for such debt.**

## What do I mean about this? ...

A debt collector must have an original copy of the original contract to prove that the debt is yours. Most of the time when a debt collector becomes abusive is because they know they don't have real proof that the debt is yours and it's their last ditch effort to try to abuse you to the point of paying the past due debt. When this type of debt collections abuse happens, it means that they bought your debt for pennies and possibly the debt can be out of Statute of Limitations.

*\* I know this very well as I've worked in collections agency and I personally have been harassed and abused by debt collectors too.*

## Things You Need To Know...

If you are being harassed by an abusive debt collector you need to know this Secret methods that are listed below so that you can give that knock out Ninja kick that will stop a debt collector.

1. **How The Collection Process Works** - You need to know if the debt collector works for the creditor or if they are a 3rd party debt buyer. A 3rd party collections agency means that they bought your debt for pennies on the dollar.

2. **Know Your Laws** - This is **very** important as you need to know the laws that protect you from abusive debt collection practices. Even if you owe the debt, a collector is required to treat you like a real human being. However, this hardly ever happens, as it's all too often that a debt collector will be very rude and treat you rudely. If you know your laws it makes it easier for you to put an end to this type of abuse.

3. **Always Ask Questions** - You need to know the Who, What, When, Where and How type of questions. When a debt collector contacts you, these are very important questions you need to ask.

    A) Who they are?

    B) What debt are they contacting you on?

    C) When did they obtain the debt?

    D) Where are they located?

    1. Address, City & State

    2. Agent's extension number & Phone Number

    E) How they obtained the debt?

You have the right to know the answer to these questions. If a debt collector fails to give you any of this information they are violating the **FDCPA,** giving you the right to sue the debt collector for violation of the FDCPA laws.

4. **Record Everything** - Whenever a debt collector contacts you its important to keep a detailed record of any by using the Log I provided for you in the previous bonus book and write down all the communication you have with the debt collector.

55

**Some of the things you need to annotate are:**

    A) Dates and Times of phone conversations.

    B) Save every voicemail the debt collector leaves.

    C) Copies of any letters you send or receive and tracking #.

    D) Names of all the collection agents you speak to.

    E) Notes of any conversation you have with a debt collector

It's important to keep track of all of this information as it could save you from getting a judgment if a debt collector tries to sue you in court. It will also help you win a case for **abusive** debt collection practices if you decide to sue a debt collector for violating your consumer rights or the **FDCPA**.

**5. Get Everything In Writing** - You should always get any type of contact from a debt collector in writing. If a debt collector calls you, ask the collections agent to send you a letter about the debt rather than talk about it on the phone. There's no doubt that the collector will try to keep you on the phone, just <u>tell them that you would prefer a letter and then hang up</u>. If you ever send a letter to the collector make sure you always send it **certified return receipt requested**, this will be your proof that the debt collector did in fact received your letter.

If you are trying to negotiate your debts with the debt collector always send a letter and <u>never make a payment arrangement or settlement with a collector over the phone</u>. If you make payment arrangements over the phone you will restart the SOL, not to mention you have a better chance of **seeing pigs fly** than you are of having the collector hold up their word, they always back out. Even if you do manage to get a collector to hold up their end of the agreement it will be like pulling a nail with your teeth.

6. **Clarify Payments** - Whenever you make a payment arrangement or negotiate a debt it's extremely important to know what debt the payments go to. This is especially important if you have more than one debt with the same debt collector.

Always get your payment arrangements in writing and make sure specify which debt each payment is going to. If the debt collector doesn't put it in writing make sure you send a letter to the debt collector **specifying** which debt you want your payments to go to and then keep track of your payments.

7. **Don't Be Bullied** - Never get bullied into paying a debt you don't own or that you have no knowledge of. Never make a payment to a debt collector unless you have sent them a debt validation letter first, you need proof that the debt is yours. Remember if a debt collector doesn't have proof of the debt then you don't owe it and it can be removed from your credit report.

8. **Don't Overpay** - Sometimes when a debt collector buys a debt they will add on interest along with a whole long list of other fees. You need to make sure they aren't over pay and never pay any more than you originally owed.

If you don't know how much that amount was, you can call the original creditor, they will be able to tell you. Just keep in mind that if the debt is with a debt collector, you may have to pay the collector rather than the original creditor.

If you can get the original creditor to take a settlement and they are willing to delete the account, it is better to pay the original creditor. If the debt collector want paid they will take the original amount not less. If they argue about it, <u>hang up</u> and make them think you are not going to pay. Send them a letter in a month or two with a settlement offer, like for example 45% off the original debt, after a while you will find that they will eventually give in and take what you are offering them, rather than risking not getting paid at all.

9. **Always File Complaints** - If an abusive debt collector is harassing you, do not be afraid to file a complaint with the FTC as well as your states Attorney General. If a debt collector still continues to harass and abuse you, do not be afraid to file a lawsuit against them as you can get up to **$1,000** plus attorney's fees. Remember debt collectors are abusive because a majority of the time **no one makes a complaint against them.**

10. **Seek Help** - Sometimes you just need help and when you do it is always a **good idea to seek help**. If you need legal advice talk to an attorney even if you don't plan on retaining one as they can often point you in the right direction.

You can also seek help from Consumer Credit Counseling Services to help you setup a budget and repayment plan if you are thinking about bankruptcy.

11. **Never Ignore A Debt Collector** - Even though some debt collectors can be abusive it's never a good idea to completely ignore them, even if the debt isn't yours. The reason for this is that you don't want a debt collector to end up taking you to court and obtaining a judgment just because you ignored them. It's better to respond, **find out the nature of the debt** and then take the **proper action** against the collector to keep them from becoming abusive.

12. **Keep Your Personal Information Safe** - Believe it or not there are a **lot of fake debt collectors out there that will scam you out of your hard earned cash**. Which is why you should **never give out your Social Security number our your bank or credit card information**. If it's a legitimate debt collector they will already have this information and there is no reason you should ever have to give it out.

   \* All too often a **fake debt collector** will **ask you** for that information and they will tell you it's for **security** purposes. Regardless of what they tell you **never give your personal information out**. Instead give them your name and the address. Remember the last thing you want is to wake up to an empty bank account, a maxed out credit card or worse being the victim of identity theft.

13. **You Have The Right To Privacy** - A debt collector **is not** allowed to share your information with friends, family, your employer or any other person or entity. A debt collector must make sure your information is safe. They are also **not allowed** to tell anyone that they are trying to collect on a debt. If a debt collector calls anyone other than yourself, they are only allowed to ask how they can get a hold of you. If a debt collector has your contact information they are not allowed to call anyone other than you.

If a debt collector has your contact information and they call your friends, family, employer they are **violating the FDCPA,** you can make a complaint with the **FTC** and your State's Attorney General and you can to file a lawsuit against the debt collector.

14. **Send A Cease & Desist Letter** - If you are constantly getting calls at home or work you can always send a Cease & Desist letter to the debt collector. Usually a Cease & Desist letter will keep the collector from calling you constantly.

You have the right under the FDCPA to stop any further phone calls. If you send a Cease & Desist letter to a debt collector and they **fail to stop calling** they are in **violation** of the FDCPA and you can take them to court and get an award of up to **$1,000** plus attorney's fees. If the debt collector is calling you on a cell phone a verbal cease & desists is all you need to stop the debt collector cold. Just make sure you annotate the time & date of the phone call and the name of the collection agency and the person you talked to.

15. **Calls From Law Enforcement Agencies** - If you get calls from someone claiming to be from a law enforcement agency or process server **never give out any information** not even an address. The reason for this is because a legitimate law enforcement agency will never, ever call you regarding a debt, it's **not their job** and owing a debt is not a crime.

If you get a call about a debt from someone claiming to be with a law enforcement agency, it is always a **fake debt collector** that is out to **steal** your hard earned cash and possibly even your identity.

16. **Debts Not Covered By The FDCPA** - Yes it's true not all debts are covered by the FDCPA. Some of the types of debt that are not covered are:

    A) **Firs Party Creditors** - First party creditors are basically the original creditor or lender and they are not bound by the **FDCPA**. However most of them will follow some of the basic guidelines setup by the **FDCPA** that means they will not call you before 8:00am or after 9:00pm as a courtesy but if they wanted to call you earlier they can.

    B) **Internal Revenue Service** - The **IRS** as well as your States Department IRS is not required to follow FDCPA rules. If you owe a debt to your State or Federal government they can contact you anyway, even if it means showing up on your doorstep.

If you owe a debt to your state or the IRS it's wise to **seek help from a licensed attorney** as they can often negotiate a reasonable payment arrangement for you.

C.) **Student Loan Guarantors** - If you are past due on a student loan or are the co-signer on a student loan any lender for a student loan is also not covered under the FDCPA. It's always a good idea to make a payment arrangement or ask for a hardship extension as student loans do not have Statute of Limitations which means a past due student loan will remain on your credit report until It's paid in full.

* If you are filing for bankruptcy you can't include any Student loan debt in your bankruptcy so you will still be responsible for the student loan debt even after you file for bankruptcy.

* However, if you are suffering a financial hardship due to a permanent disability and your Doctor can prove you cannot go back to school or work due to that disability then you can have any student loans that you have removed completely. If this is your situation contact your lender they will provide you with the forms and the details of their process to remove the debt.

17. **Attorneys Are Subject To The FDCPA** - If you ever get a call from an attorney or attorney's office to collect on a past due debt. They must follow the rules covered in the FDCPA. Never let someone from an attorney's office bully you into paying, especially if you have no knowledge of the debt or you believe the debt isn't yours. It's all too often that collectors calling from attorney's office will claim they don't have to follow the FDCPA because they are in a legal office.

An attorney and their debt collectors should know that they **must** follow the FDCPA.

Before you give any information to someone claiming to be from an attorney's office you can always **contact the American Bar Association** to find out if they are **licensed to collect in your State**. If they are not listed with the American Bar Association **don't give out any** information, there are **fake collectors** who claims to be an attorney just to get your info.

18. **Always Validate The Debt** – It is important to **validate any and all debts** with every debt collector that contacts you before you make any type of payment arrangement. You need to know if the debt belongs to you and if it's within the Statute of Limitations also they **need to show** written documentation to prove the debt is yours. The documentation is often a written or signed contract by you. A letter of the debt collector's letterhead with the amount owed **is not sufficient enough evidence** to hold up in court **as verifiable proof.**

**If you know and understand these "Secret" rules before a debt collector contacts you about a past due debt, you will be able to give the collector a powerful Ninja kick and knock them out!**

# Chapter 11
# Guide to Being Judgment Proof

*In this chapter we show you the Ninja's guide to keeping your assets safe...*

In today's economy it's easy to fall a little behind on your obligations. Sometimes bad things happen to good people; whatever your situation is it's not something that happen by choice. Whether you have fallen behind because of a job loss, divorce, illness in the family, or just plain had a streak of bad luck. Whatever your situation is you may find yourself being harassed and abused by an abusive debt collector who is threatening to take you to court to obtain a judgment. If you find yourself in this situation you can Ninja kick your debt collectors in the face.

# What Happens If A Collector Obtains A Judgment?

You should always try to avoid a judgment but sometimes things happen to good people no matter how much we try to avoid it. If a debt collector is able to obtain a judgment against you is never fun, as they can literally make your life a living hell and I do mean that literally.

When a debt collector has a judgment you can't just get them to go away. Even if you send them a cease and desist all you will be able to do is to stop them from calling but it won't make your debt collection nightmare go away as they have the upper hand.

When a debt collector obtains a judgment against you, they have a long list of abusive debt collection practices that will allow them to collect on the debt. If you find yourself in this position you can become judgment proof.

## What does it mean to have judgment?

It means that a debt collector with a judgment can do lots of damage to your credit report since this will show up in your credit report and drop your score from 100 points or more depending on the type of judgment. They can also cause financial damage, loss of property, and emotional damage due to the stress caused to by utilizing all the abusive techniques to force you to pay the debt.

Before we go into… How to protect yourself and make your assets judgment proof, you first need to understand the different ways in which a debt collector can collect when they have a judgment against you.

**When a debt collector has a judgment against you they can collect on the judgment by using one of the following abusive but yet legal collection methods:**

1. **Garnish Your Wages** - This is one of the most popular and common methods that a debt collector will use in order to collect. If this happens to you it could literally cause you to be short on other bills and can put you further behind making you subject to possibly further harassment by another debt collector or even worse another judgment.

2. **Seize Your Property** - Depending on your State's laws a debt collector can seize your property or place a lien against your property. This helps the debt collector as they can sell your property to repay the debt or if they have a lien against your property it means that you can't sell the property until the judgment is satisfied or paid. The types of property commonly targeted are usually property such as real estate like land or a house if not your car is usually the next item on the list to be seized. Anything that you own with any real value can be used to pay back the loan. Jewelry, coins, other collectibles, expensive animals or have liens placed against them. Yes! If you have an expensive pet loan, your pet can be a debt collector's ticket to repay your debt.

3. **Levy Your Bank Account** – If you have a judgment against you it is legal for a debt collector to levy your bank account, if they know where you bank. A court will notify you before a bank levy can occur but if you don't respond to the paperwork or you simply never got a copy of the judgment or the request to levy your bank accounts; this means that you could literally wake up one day to a completely empty bank account and there will be absolutely nothing you can do about it once it happens.

The bad part about a bank levy is that it could cause you to be late on your car payments, your mortgage or rent payments. I've seen a bank levy completely put a person on the street. I've even seen small children go hungry because their parents had their accounts levied. It's sad and I don't think a debt collector should ever be allowed to levy a person's bank account. But the law allows it if a court grants a debt collectors request to levy your bank accounts. The upside to it is that a court usually won't grant a levy unless the debt collector has exhausted all other collection methods.

## What Does It Mean To Be Judgment Proof?

Judgment proofing yourself simply means that a debt collector can't use any of the above dirty little tricks to take your assets to collect on the debt. Sometimes people tend to think that if they are judgment proof it means that a debt collector can't sue them in court so that they can obtain a judgment against the debtor. If you're in this category we need to erase that from your mind, as **it is absolutely incorrect**. Just because you are judgment proof still doesn't keep a debt collector from obtaining a judgment, as they can. It only means that they can't garnish your wages, seize your property or levy your bank accounts.

The truth of the matter is if you don't take the necessary steps to make sure your assets are judgment proof you might as well be playing Russian roulette with a loaded gun hoping the gun never goes off. But just like Russian roulette, the gun will eventually go off and when it does you will find yourself floating face down dead in the water.

Yes, I know that sounds harsh! But don't worry you won't actually die as that was just a <u>figure of speech</u> as that is exactly how you will feel, dead floating face down in the water especially if you have your wages garnished or your bank account levied and you find yourself not being able to pay the rest of your bills. It is not something you will want to go through, so you should try to avoid having that happen to you, like the plague by working with your debt collectors before it gets to that point.

I know you may be thinking that a debt collector can't levy your bank account or seize any of your other assets, as they don't know where you bank or what type of assets you own. The truth of the matter is that debt collectors know the inside **secrets to finding this information out**. So, before you think you can run across home plate safe and clear you might want to think again as the ball might already be waiting to tag you before you reach home plate.

## How Does A Collector Find And Seize My Home?

In today's society and with the advancement of computers and social websites like Facebook, LinkedIn, Twitter along with a bunch of other sites on the Internet it makes it easier than ever for a debt collector to find your valuable assets. It's not un-heard of for a debt collector to search online databases to find out where you live, work and in some cases even where you bank. If you own a home or other types of real estate it's extremely easy to do a title search since this information is readily available to the public by searching the property tax assessor's office.

The fact is that most States counties have websites for the County Property Tax Assessor's Office. On these same sites you will usually find a public database that can be searched to find out if you own any type of real estate. As wrong as that is it is public information and anyone with a computer, or smart phone and an Internet connection can find the title to any property you may have. Which makes any real estate you own easy to locate and seize or have a lien placed against it, which would force you to pay the lien before you could sell your property.

## Can A Collector Find My Bank Account?

If you have judgment that was filed against you by a debt collector your bank account could be levied. A bank levy is when a debt collector takes a lump sum payment out of your bank account to help pay back your debt. Sometimes this will drain a person's entire bank account or sometimes less, it depends on how much the debt was for. A debt collector who has a judgment against you can levy your account for the full balance of the debt. As cruel as this collection tactic may be it is legal, as the courts will allow a debt collector to levy a person's bank account.

\* This practice can cause a snowball effect which could easily cause you to miss your car payment, utilities, keep you from buying food or even cause you to miss your mortgage or rent payment, which could cause you to end up in a position where you find yourself homeless. Believe it or not this happens to people on a daily basis as they find themselves having to skip other bills to make up for the ones they no longer can pay because of the bank levy.

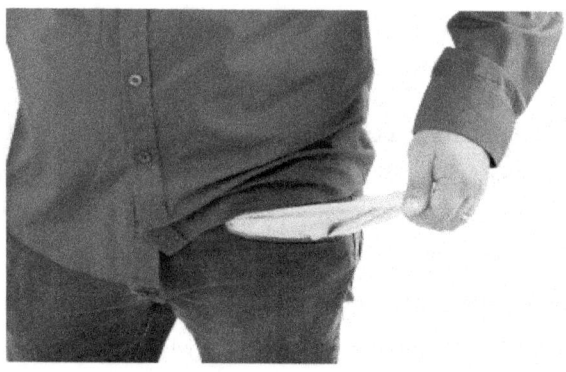

This is also where predatory lending like payday loans comes into play as it is sometimes the only option for some people to pay the necessary bills that keep a roof over their head and food on their tables.

A bank levy is never a fun experience and I hope you never end up in this situation. A court will usually never grant a bank levy unless the debt collector has tried every other option available to them, which include wage garnishments and property seizure. But if none of those options are available or have not worked for the debt collector the courts will grant a levy to a debt collector, which is why **you need to be aware of them.**

I personally don't think this should be a legal tactic, but nonetheless it is a legal tactic and there are a bunch of ways that a debt collector can find out where and how you bank.

**Let's take a look at some of the methods that are used by a debt collector to find out your personal information including your bank account.**

1. **Making Payment Arrangements** - If you have a judgment against you and you decide to make a payment towards the debt with a check, bank debit card or online you have just set yourself up for a bank levy. Why? because now the collector knows you have money to make payments, causing them to levy your bank account to pay off the debt faster. It's not a good idea to make a payment to a collector unless you're using a money order or other types of payment methods like Western Union or Money Gram. **I'm not saying don't make payments**, I'm just saying <u>**do not use a check, bank transfer or a payment with your bank debit card.**</u> The best option is to pay with a money order.

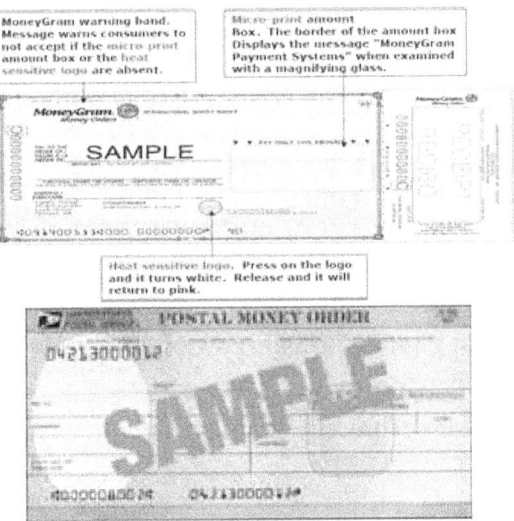

The **money order** stub is your proof that the payment was made. Make copies and always send the payment by certified return receipt requested. This can be expensive, but it will save you a big headache if your bank accounts were to be levied.

2. **Court Order** - Whenever a judgment is filed against you the court can force you to fill out a form that lists all of your monthly expenses and banking information. A debt collector will use this tactic to garnish your wages. If the debt collector is not able to collect through wage garnishment because you don't have a job or are paid in another method, the debt collector will use the information that you submitted to the court to obtain a bank levy as the debt collector is usually provided with a copy of the information you submitted to the court. This also sets you up for a possible bank levy if the debt collector is unable to garnish your wages. Keep in mind if the court requires you to submit your financial information, you must provide the information. If you leave off your banking information and the courts learn later that you had a bank account they will find you in contempt of court, which could lead to possible jail time. **Very important is that you always be truthful when providing this information to the courts**.

3. **You Cash A Check** – Yes! I did say that, cashing a check from a debt collector could be harmful to your bank account. If you have a judgment against you and the debt collector doesn't know where you bank, they could still find it. I know you are probably wondering how they would find it if you never provided them with that information and the courts didn't require you to provide your bank information.

**Debt collectors will sometimes send you a check usually of no more than $1.00 to $5.00 with a letter** stating that you paid more than the required amount or they over charged you on interest. Believe it or not this happens a lot and most people usually fall for it due to the fact that sometimes a few dollars can go a long way towards making ends meet.

That's exactly what the debt collector is hoping for when they send you the check as <u>they are counting on the fact that you will go to your bank to cash or deposit the check and when you do, they will get a copy of the canceled check which then tells them where you bank as well as your account number</u>. When this happens a debt collector is trying to find your bank information out so they can levy your account.

# Judgment Proofing Yourself

Even though a debt collector can take you to court and obtain a judgment on any past due debts that you owe, it doesn't always mean that they will be able to collect.

Yes! You can legally become judgment proof. I know you are probably thinking… **How do I become judgment proof?**

In order to be judgment proof you have to qualify for what's called a **Judgment Exemption** is when you meet certain requirements that keep a debt collector from collecting on any judgment they own for your past due debt. Keep in mind that just because <u>you become judgment proof doesn't mean that a debt collector won't take you to court to obtain a judgment</u> as a **collector can still take you to court.**

# What Exemptions Are Available

When a debt collector obtains a judgment you can claim a judgment exemption that will help keep a debt collector from garnishing your wages or levy your bank account.

**Some of the exemptions that you can claim include:**

1. Alimony
2. Retirement Pensions
3. Workers Compensation
4. Student Financial Aid
5. Unemployment Benefits
6. Military Veteran's Benefits
7. Child Support
8. Social Security
9. SSI Payments

If you have any of these types of incomes you can claim an exemption, which means that the debt collector will not be able to garnish these types of incomes.

**Keeping Your Property Safe**

If you think that you are going to be sued by a debt collector, there are simple Secrets that every Credit Ninja should know to keep their property safe from being seized by a debt collector. I know you are probably thinking what Credit Ninja Secrets will allow me to become a Ninja Warrior to fight the evil debt collector horde?

# Chapter 12

# Let's look at some of these different ways to protect your assets using this Credit Ninja Secret Methods...

## Protecting Your Income

Wage garnishment is usually the first tactic a debt collector will use to collect on a judgment. If you have a job and have been working at the same place for a while you can count on having your wages garnished. Currently there are four States that don't allow a debt collector to garnish wages, which are **Texas, Pennsylvania, South Carolina,** and **North Carolina.** If you live in one of these States chances are that you will probably never have to worry about having your wages garnished.

**But, What happens if you don't live in one of the four States? There are several ways that you can do to avoid having your wages garnished.**

1. **Job Hopping** - This tactic involves changing jobs frequently which keeps a debt collector from ever being able to garnish your wages. I don't really ever recommend anyone doing this, but I have seen it done. If you find yourself in a position of ever having your wages garnished it could be a useful tactic.

*Job-hopping works because whenever a debt collector notifies your employer of a wage garnishment you have to be served paperwork that tells you when your wage garnishment will begin. When this happens you can leave your job and find new employment, as <u>it will take a debt collector 6 months to a year to find your new employment</u>.

People who use this tactic usually do this till the Statute of Limitations runs out or the judgment expires. However, **I don't recommend doing or using** these tactics as it's always better to pay your debts, but it's not illegal to do if you decide to use this tactic. I've seen a lot of debtors use this tactic and it's actually very effective if you don't mind changing jobs once or twice a year.

2. **Work In Canada or Mexico** - If you live near the Canadian or Mexican borders you can always obtain a job across the border. I know that sounds bad but it is legal. There are no laws that say you can't commute across the border on a daily basis if you live near one of these two countries. I'm not sure how much a company in Mexico pays their employees; Canada would probably make a better choice but it could be done.

Here's how this tactic works. You live near the border for one of these countries. You would find a job in that country, buy land and become a resident even though you still live in the States.

When you have <u>income and land in another country a debt collector will never be able to levy that property or garnish your wages because is out of their jurisdiction and a court would never grant a levy or lien on property that is located in another country</u>.

3. **Cash Only Income** – Let's face it, there isn't a lot of jobs on the market these days that pay cash however it doesn't mean you can't find a job that pays you cash. If you're extremely handy you can always become a handyman and do odd jobs and get paid by cash only. <u>Having a **cash only income** is a sure fire way to Ninja knock out your debt collectors, I like it so much as it's not illegal to have a cash only income.</u>

If you were going to have a cash only income it would be a good idea to try and pay for everything in cash rather than obtaining a loan or using a credit card. I know it's not always easy to pay for everything in cash especially in this day and age but it will keep your income safe from having your wages garnished.

4. **Deductions** - If you have a job that you don't want to leave, you can still possibly avoid wage garnishment depending on how much is your weekly take home pay is. Most States are only allowed to garnish your wages up to certain percentage of your paycheck. In Missouri 25% of total disposable income can be garnished. The disposable income is what you take home minus any expenses that are exempt from being garnished. The more you have taken out of your paycheck it will reduce the amount that is garnished out of the paycheck. Sometimes if you have enough deductions taken out you can avoid wage garnishment all together, if your paycheck is lower than $217.50 which is the Federal limit on wage garnishments. This tactic works if you have the deductions come out of your check. Some of these deductions can include child support, alimony, taxes and any other deductions.

You can also increase the amount you have withheld for your Federal and State taxes that will come back to you when you file your yearly taxes assuming you don't owe the IRS any back taxes. So, if you don't mind forgoing a few extra luxuries during the year you could find yourself enjoying a nice tax return, which you can use to help catch up on the or simply save it for a rainy day.

Either way this will help you reduce the amount that you can have garnished or it will help you avoid wage garnishments. For this tactic I would recommend that you **seek the advice of a licensed attorney or accountant** to find out what type of deductions you can have taken out of your paycheck.

**Department of Labor** - This website http://www.dol.gov/ has a fact sheet that talks about the Federal wage garnishment limits.

# Avoiding A Bank Levy

As you know having a bank levied by a debt collector **can be financially devastating** for any family and could cause your ship to sink. Let's face it; no one wants his or her boat to sink.

**There are a few ways that you can keep your bank account from being levied:**

1. **Check Cashing** - As I mentioned earlier on in this book some debt collectors will send you a check for a small amount in hopes that you will walk right down to the bank and cash it. If you do that, the debt collector will find your account, as the cancelled check will tell them where you bank and your bank account will be at risk of a levy.

I've had debt collectors try to use this tactic on me however due to the fact that I am an ex-collection agent, I am already familiar with this tactic and I have been known to send the checks back to the debt collector which really irritates them. However, if you need the cash and those few dollars make a difference in your finances use a check cashing service, which you can find almost anywhere these days. I know Wal-Mart will cash most checks for a fee of course. Keep in mind that most check cashing places including Wal-Mart will charge a fee, which can add up, but it's much cheaper than what it would cost you if your bank were levied.

2. **Online Banking** - It's pretty hard for a debt collector to find out where you bank without taking extra measures to protect your account from a bank levy. But if you live in a small town, most debt collectors will serve every bank in town a bank levy order in hopes that they will get a direct hit and find your bank account. I've heard of people do their banking in another State, which is perfectly legal to do.

Example: John lives in Florida but his bank account is in Alaska chances are the debt collector would have an extremely hard time locating John's bank account. In this day and age there are a lot of online banks that offer really nice rates. Since online banks are exactly just that, it's extremely hard for a debt collector to levy your account.

3. **Offshore Banking** - If you do all of your banking offshore then you are pretty much safe from having your bank account levied as they can't levy an account that is in another country. However, you can still have your offshore bank account levied if you owe State or Federal taxes and they don't have to sue you to obtain a judgment, they can simply levy your account regardless of where in the world your bank account is located. Having an offshore account is a great way to protect your assets. However before you run out and obtain an offshore account I would recommend that you speak with a **licensed attorney or your accountant** as having an offshore account is legal it does have its pros and cons just like anything else.

One of the biggest things to remember about a bank levy is that a debt collector can only levy a bank account that they can find. Keep in mind that it <u>is illegal to hide your bank account from a debt collector if they already have a judgment against you</u>. It is not illegal to take the extra precaution to make sure your bank account is protected **before** a judgment is filed against you.

## Avoiding Property Liens

If you own a home or have any other type of property such as land or a car, a debt collector can put a lien on any type of property you own. If a debt collector has a judgment against you they can put a lien against your property or they can foreclose on your home or repossess your car.

1. **Home and Auto Payments** - If you have a home or auto loan it could help you avoid having a lien placed against your home or auto. The reason for this is that a debt collector will have to pay money out of pocket to have a lien placed against your home or auto with little or no chance of recovering the expenses they put out. One of the reason for that is, if you are making payments on your home or auto the debt collector will have to pay off the balance for your mortgage or auto loan before they can keep any of the cash from the sale of your property.

**Example:** You have a $150,000 mortgage and you owe $145,000 and you have a judgment against you for $20,000 would leave you with $5,000 in equity which is much less than the $20,000 owed to the debt collector.

Keep in mind that the debt collector has to pay off your mortgage of $145,000 before they can collect on the remaining equity of $5,000 and after court costs and all the other fees they will spend about another $5,000 just to obtain an amount that was less than the amount owed.

This is not really a profitable scenario for the debt collector which means that the chances of them foreclosing on your property is extremely unlikely and here is why:

After the sale of your house and after the debt collector pays the $145,000 remaining balance they would have $5,000 left over to go towards the debt that you owe which brings the balance you owe down to $15,000 and they spent $5,000 to foreclose on the home which would still leave the debt collector in the hole for the same $20,000 that you originally owed. I can't think of any debt collector that will try to foreclose on your property with this type of scenario.

Now you're probably wondering when it is a viable and profitable option for a debt collector to foreclose on your property. Let's take the same scenario above but change it around some in the example below you will be able to see the different scenario.

**Example:** You have a $150,000 mortgage and you still owe $115,000 on your mortgage, which would give you $35,000 in equity. This scenario would be profitable if the debt collector were to foreclose on your property.

They would be able to pay off the mortgage for $115,000 and after they pay the $20,000 they would still come out with an extra $15,000 in profit, as they would be allowed to keep the rest the remaining balance. The law doesn't require a debt collector to pay you the remaining balance of $15,000 as they had the right to foreclose which means anything left over is theirs to keep free and clear.

As you can tell it's not always profitable for a debt collector to foreclose or repossess your property, which is why it's sometimes better to continue making payments on your mortgage or auto loan rather than pay the house or car off early.

If you own your home and you don't have a mortgage or you don't have an auto loan on your car and a debt <u>collector places a lien on your property you can count on losing your home or auto to foreclosure or repossession from a debt collector even if you are current on your payments.</u>

2. **Taking Out A 2nd Loan** - Sometimes having <u>more than one lien holder on your property can be a great way to keep your property from being foreclosed</u> on due to the fact that the debt collector would have to pay off both loans before they can apply any remaining balance towards your debt.

In other words if you have more than one loan on your home or auto you are probably upside down which means there is no possibly way for a debt collector to collect on the debt if they foreclose since there would be no equity left over after they pay off both of the loans that you have on your home or auto. I have seen people take out a loan from friends and family which then creates a 2nd lien holder.

The way this works is that a friend or family member gives you a small loan and then <u>you have them added to the title of your home or auto</u> which will keep a debt collector from foreclosing on your home or auto since there is a second lien holder.

I am not saying that you should go out and do this as you will have an extra payment each month to your normal expenses but there is no law that states you can't take out a second loan on your home or auto.

# CHAPTER 13
# Simple Guide to Credit Disputes

In this chapter you will learn the exact step to take when sending credit disputes and how to keep track of all of your disputes. Keeping track of your disputes is extremely important to anyone who is trying to repair their credit files.

If you don't keep track of your files properly you are setting yourself up for credit suicide, as the debt collector will have an advantage if they decide to ever take you to court.

When you keep track of your credit disputes and a debt collector takes you to court chances are the judge will rule in your favor if you have a detailed record of all your disputes along with a detailed log of any phone conversations you have with a debt collector along with the dates, time called, phone number and a brief summary of the conversation.

## Record Keeping

Before you begin disputing information in your credit file or validate a debt with any debt collector, you need to have a system set up that will allow you to easily manage and keep track of all of the letters you send out along with any phone conversations with a debt collector regardless if they call you or you call them.

Keeping track of calls is a vital step that you cannot miss. I usually have several folders that I use to keep track of everything. Keep in mind this system may not work for everyone as everyone has his or her own way to keep track of information.

If you have a different method that is okay as long as you are keeping track of everything. Here is how my tracking system is setup.

1. In my computer have *3 separate folders, 1 for each Credit Bureau*. In each folder I will put copies of dispute letters that I have sent to them, copies of the certified return receipt to prove they received the letter along with copies of any updated credit reports that they send me.

2. I also have 1 folder for each debt collector. In each folder I will put copies of the debt validation letters, cease and desist letters. Also I scan my proof the letters that were mailed and received, phone conversations, log of all calls and any other type of communication with debt collectors. All mentioned above will go in that folder so that way if I have to sue a collector for violating both State and Federal laws or they end up taking me to court I have a detailed record of everything.

# Document Preparation

**Step 1:** A type written letter is good but handwriting is good too.

**Step 2:** Sign the letters; it looks more professional and will show the credit bureau or the collector that you mean business.

**Step 3:** Make 3 copies of any letter you send along with anything you attach to the letters.

> **A.** You will keep a copy for your records. Keep the originals to send to a credit bureau or collector.
>
> **B.** You will send a copy to the debt collector.
>
> **C.** You will also keep a copy back to submit to the court if you ever have to sue a credit bureau or debt collector.

**Step 4:** Make sure you have the correct Address on the envelope.

**Step 5:** Go to your Post Office or anywhere that you go to send your mail and purchase the green Certified Return Receipt Requested label. By doing this the other party must sign it certifying that they received your letter. The Post Office will send the signed green card back for your records.

**Step: 6** Send the letter and wait for a response from the collector or credit bureau.

# Maintaining Your Records

For every letter you send to a creditor, debt collector, or credit bureau you need to have all of the following documents in the corresponding folder. Here is a list of what should go in each folder for every letter you send.

1. Original copies of each letter you send with any attachments stapled to the letter.

2. Receipt from purchasing the postage for each letter. If you have more than one letter try to do separate transactions for each one or staple the receipt to each letter and highlight the postage for that letter if you have more than one letter on that same receipt.

3. A signed copy of the Certified Return Receipt when it gets sent back to you.

4. A communication log with the date, time, along with whom the letter was mailed to.

You need to keep the folders in a safe place as you should keep copies of everything for 10 years to make sure none of the collection accounts are put back on your credit file. If this happens you will have proof of everything.

Make sure you do this for every letter you send including when you make a payment. Having a record of everything not only can help you avoid a judgment, it will also help increase and maintain your credit score as it will make it harder for collection accounts to be put back on. If they somehow appear back in your credit report you will be able to use this information to sue the collector, credit bureau in the event it shows back up and they refuse to remove it.

## Important Resources

Here are a few important resources to sites that can be used to help you better understand the laws that will help you become a Credit Ninja Warrior and Ninja Kick your way to better credit report.

**FTC** - The Federal Trade Commission has form that will allow you to file a complaint against any collector that isn't following the FDCPA & FCRA laws. (www.ftccomplaintassistant.gov)

**FDCPA** - Here you will find a full copy of the Fair Debt Collection Practices Act that will help you understand the some of the things that protect you from abusive debt collection practices. (www.consumer.ftc.gov/articles/pdf-0097-fair-debt-collection-practices-act.pdf)

**FCRA** - Here you will find a copy of the Fair Credit Reporting Act that regulates how information is reported on your credit report. (www.ftc.gov/os/statutes/031224fcra.pdf)

**CFPB** - The Consumer Financial Protection Bureau helps regulate and enforce laws that affect the financial industry as a whole, which includes creditors, collection agencies, banks, credit repair agencies and other institutions. If you think you're being discriminated or simply being harassed by a debt collector then you should file a complaint with the CFPB. (www.consumerfinance.gov)

**UCCC** - Uniform Consumer Credit Code - This federal statue became a law by the National Conference of Commissioners in 1968. This statue protects consumers from the illegal charging of high interest rates and limits creditors from using state courts to gain access to a debtors assets or the garnishing of wages. (/www.uniformlaws.org/shared/docs/Consumer Credit Code/UCCC1974.pdf)

**ECOA** - Equal Credit Opportunity Act - This act regulates the discrimination of credit applicants based on sex, religion, race, sex and a whole long list of other discrimination tactics that a lender could use against an applicant. (www.fdic.gov/regulations/laws/rules/6500-200.html#fdic65001002.4)

**SCRA** - Service Members Civil Relief Act was put into place to protect military members who are on active duty during war or any other active military duty from being harassed by abusive debt collectors. However this act protects service members in many different ways besides just credit. (http://www.servicememberscivilreliefact.com/link/text-of-act.php)

These are just some of the resources that will help you become a true Ninja Credit Warrior.

# Credit Form Letters

In the following pages you will find letters that I used to dispute, correct and repair my credit. Feel free to edit and use the following sample letters that are included in this book.

These letters are to be sent out to the credit bureaus and collection agencies. Keep in mind that it is best if you use the appropriate letter according to the situation you are disputing, don't forget to use the steps mentioned in the chapters above.

# The Credit Ninja

*This letter is to be sent when you don't want a debt collector to call you or your employer. Once a debt collector receives this letter they are no longer allowed to contact you by phone, they will only be allowed to contact you via regular mail.*

Date:_____

Your Name
1234 Family Street
Hometown, MO 64118

To: ABC Collections Company
    1234 Harassment Street
    Collectors, N.Y. 10022

Hello ABC Collections Company,

I am writing in response to your constant phone calls! **According to the Fair Debt Collection Practices Act,** (15 USC 1692c) Section 805(c): **CEASING COMMUNICATION:** You must cease all communication with me after being notified in writing that I no longer wish to communicate with you. Therefore, I demand that you stop calling me at home, work, my cell phone or at any other location!

In accordance with the federal **FDCPA**, now that you have received this "stop calling" letter, you may only contact me by mail to inform me that you:

- Are terminating further collection efforts;
- Invoking specified remedies which are ordinarily invoked by you or your company; or
- Intend to invoke a specified remedy.

Be advised that I am well aware of my rights! For example, I know that any future contact by you or your company violates the FDCPA and that since you already have my location information, calls made by you or your company to any 3rd party concerning me violates section **805(b) 2 of the FDCPA.** In addition be advised that I am keeping accurate records of all correspondence from you and your company; including recording all phone calls. If you continue calling me I will pursue all available legal actions to stop you from harassing my family and me.

Sincerely,

*Your Signature*

Your Name

This letter is to be sent when you don't want a debt collector to call you or your employer. Once a debt collector receives this letter they are no longer allowed to contact you by phone, they will only be allowed to contact you via regular mail.

Date:_____

Your Name
1234 Family Street
Hometown, MO 64118

To: ABC Collections Company
    1234 Harassment Street
    Collectors, N.Y. 10022

Hello ABC Collections Company,

I am writing in response to your constant phone calls that are in violation of the **Fair Debt Collection Practices Act**, specifically:

**804(3) - Acquisition of Location Information (15 USC 1692b)**: Any debt collector communicating with any person other than the consumer for the purpose of acquiring location information about the consumer shall not communicate with any such person <u>more than once</u> unless requested to do so by such person or unless the debt collector reasonably believes that the earlier response of such person is erroneous or incomplete and that such person now has correct or complete location information.

**806(5) - Harassment or Abuse (15 USC 1692d)**: A debt collector may not engage in any conduct the natural consequence of which is to <u>harass, oppress, or abuse any person</u> in connection with the collection of a debt. The following conduct is a violation of this section; "Causing a telephone to ring or engaging any person in telephone conversation repeatedly or continuously with intent to annoy, abuse, or harass any person at the called number."

I have informed you on several occasions that the consumer you are trying to contact does not live at my address, is not associated with my phone number and that I have no additional information to provide you. Therefore, in accordance with section **804(3)**, I demand that you stop calling me at home, work, cell phone or at any other location! Be advised that I am keeping accurate records of all correspondence from you and your company; including recording all phone calls. If you continue calling me, I will consider your actions in violation of section **806(5)** and pursue all available legal actions to stop you from harassing my family and me.

Sincerely,

*Your Signature*

Your Name

This letter is to be sent to the credit bureaus when you want to dispute any collection account that's on your credit report. When you dispute an item on your report the debt will either come back as verified or deleted. If it comes back verified then you want to send a letter to find out what verification method was used to verify the debt.

Note: Make sure you include a copy of your State issued ID, as the Credit Bureaus need this to make sure you're the one requesting your Credit rather than someone else. Make sure to select the correct Credit Bureau and address that you are sending the letter to by looking at the table below.

Date:_____

Your Name
1234 Family Street
Hometown, MO 64118

| Equifax | Experian | Trans Union |
|---|---|---|
| P.O. Box 740241 | P.O. Box 2014 | P.O. Box 1000 |
| Atlanta, GA 30374 | Allen, TX 75013 | Chester, PA 19022 |

Hello Equifax (Experian or Trans Union),

I applied for a loan last week and was told that my credit scores were too low. I requested my credit reports and after reviewing them I have noticed numerous errors. I am certain this is not normal. Please correct the following errors as soon as possible.

List the addresses, wrong accounts, Public record, Judgments & Errors:
1. _____
2. _____
3. _____

If any of these accounts are verified, please provide me with the name and address of the verifying party, the method of verification, and the reported first delinquency from the original creditor otherwise please delete them from my credit file as per the **FCRA** and **FDCPA**.

Thank you for your time.

Sincerely,

*Your Signature*

Your Name
S.S.#____-__-____
DOB:____/___/___

This letter is to be sent to the credit bureaus when you want to dispute any collection account that's on your credit report. When you dispute an item on your report the debt will either come back as verified or deleted. If it comes back verified then you want to send a letter to find out what verification method was used to verify the debt.

Note: Make sure you include a copy of your State issued ID, as the Credit Bureaus need this to make sure you're the one requesting your Credit rather than someone else. Make sure to select the correct Credit Bureau and address that you are sending the letter to by looking at the table below.

Date:_____

Your Name
1234 Family Street
Hometown, MO 64118

| Equifax | Experian | Trans Union |
|---|---|---|
| P.O. Box 740241 | P.O. Box 2014 | P.O. Box 1000 |
| Atlanta, GA 30374 | Allen, TX 75013 | Chester, PA 19022 |

Hello Experian (Equifax or Trans Union):

Re: Inaccuracies on My Credit Report

I am writing for two (2) reasons:

1. To dispute certain information in my credit file
2. To have you investigate/re-investigate and remove inaccurate information from my Credit Report and prevent its re-insertion. The item(s) I dispute are encircled on the attached copy of the credit report and further identified by: (*identify the items by name of source, such as creditor or tax court, etc. and identify type of item, such as credit account, judgment, etc.*)

1. This item is (*inaccurate*) because (*describe what is wrong and why*). I am requesting that the item be deleted (*or whatever change you are requesting*) to correct the information. (*If you are enclosing documents such as copies of cancelled checks, court documents, send copies only, you always* **retain the** *originals*) -- *and use the following sentence.*

Enclosed are copies of the following documents supporting my position:
- 1.

Please reinvestigate this (these) matter(s) and (delete or correct) the disputed items within the time frame required by the **Fair Credit Reporting Act (FCRA)** and inform me in writing of the outcome.
Thank you for your time and consideration in this matter.

Sincerely,

*Your Signature*

Your Name

This letter is sent when you don't believe you owe the debt or you don't think that the collector doesn't have enough information to sue you in court. Keep in mind if a debt collector does not have sufficient proof of the debt and they still decide to take you to court, you need to show up and tell the judge that the collector hasn't been able to show you valid proof of this debt. Keep a copy of any letter you send to the collector as proof.

Date:_____

Your Name
1234 Family Street
Hometown, MO 64118

To: ABC Collections Company
   1234 Harassment Street
   Collectors, N.Y. 10022

RE: Account # _____

To Whom It May Concern:

I am formally requesting that you validate all trade line notations you have submitted to the three major credit-reporting agencies by ABC Collections Company for me, Your Name, **for account** # _____.

Due to possible inaccuracies in these CRA reports, I must demand that the validation I hereby lawfully request, to be in the form of a signed statement by a person with original knowledge of the debt. As it was constituted and who can testify that the debt was incurred legally, was not subsequently disputed as a result of returned, faulty, recalled consumer products, not utilized as a profit-loss tax deduction during the period it may have been payable and was not claimed as a loss with any insuring entity during the period it may have been payable.

Please be advised that I am not requesting a verification that you have my mailing address. Rather, I am requesting validation, i.e., competent evidence that I had some contractual obligation sans consumer protection encumbrance which incurred the original claims associated with this trade line. A trade line is more than just an accounting of payments on an account that may or may not exist.

It's rather a signed and dated contract showing that there was a contractual obligation to the debt that you say I owe. Per applicable State and Federal laws I'm asking that you verify the debt by showing an actual contractual obligation that has not been previously written off by the original creditor.

Per Federal and State law a collector is not allowed to collect on a debt that has been previously charged or written off. Also note that section **1681s-2(b) of the Fair Credit Reporting Act** creates a cause of action for a consumer against a furnisher of erroneous credit information **(Nelson v. Chase Manhattan).**

Please know that you have only **30 days** from the tracked and confirmed delivery of this lawful notice to either answer these demands or to remove the associated negative trade line notations from the CRA reports. Any other action may constitute evidence of your intent to abridge one or more civil or other constitutional rights.

Please be further advised that continued unsubstantiated reporting of possible inaccuracies to third parties may provide a basis for criminal complaints being filed in accordance with **FDCPA**, **FCRA**, and other Federal Statutes.

I look forward to a timely and amicable resolution to this matter.

Sincerely,

*Your Signature*

Your Name

This letter is sent when you don't believe you owe the debt or you don't think that the collector trying to collect doesn't have enough information to sue you in court. Keep in mind if a debt collector does not have sufficient proof of the debt and they still decide to take you to court you need to show up and tell the judge the collector hasn't been able to show you valid proof of this debt. Keep a copy of any letter you send to them.

Date:_____

Your Name
1234 Family Street
Hometown, MO 64118

To: ABC Collections Company
    1234 Harassment Street
    Collectors, N.Y. 10022

Re: Account #:_____

Hello ABC Collections Company,

I am writing in response to your (letter or phone call) dated {insert date}, (copy of the letter enclosed) because I do not believe I owe what you say I owe. This is the (insert the number) time I've disputed this debt. The first dispute was on {date} with {name of collection agency} and the second was on {date} with {name of collection agency}. Be advised that neither collection agency responded to my dispute. In accordance with the **Fair Debt Collection Practices Act**.

**Section 809(b) Validating Debts:**
    **(b)** If the consumer notifies the debt collector in writing within the thirty-day period described in subsection **(a)** that the debt, or any portion thereof, is disputed, or that the consumer requests the name and address of the original creditor, the debt collector shall cease collection of the debt, or any disputed portion thereof, until the debt collector obtains verification of the debt or any copy of a judgment, or the name and address of the original creditor, and a copy of such verification or judgment, or name and address of the original creditor, is mailed to the consumer by the debt collector.

I respectfully request that you provide me with the following information:

•(1) The amount of the debt;
•(2) The name of the creditor to whom the debt is owed;
•(3) Provide a verification or copy of any judgment (if applicable);
•(4) Proof that you are licensed to collect debts in (insert name of your state)

Be advised that I am fully aware of my rights under the Fair Debt Collection Practices Act and the Fair Credit Reporting Act. For instance, I know that:

- Because I have disputed this debt in writing within 30 days of receipt of your dunning notice, you must obtain verification of the debt or a copy of the judgment against me and mail these items to me at your expense.
- You cannot add interest or fees accept those allowed by the original contract or state law.
- You do not have to respond to this dispute but if you do, any attempt to collect this debt without validating it, violates the FDCPA;

Be advised that I am keeping very accurate records of all correspondence from you and your company including recording all phone calls and I will not hesitate to report violations of the law to my State Attorney General, the Federal Trade Commission and the Better Business Bureau.

I have disputed this debt; therefore, until validated you know your information concerning this debt is inaccurate. Thus, if you have already reported this debt to any credit-reporting agency (CRA) or Credit Bureau (CB) then, you must immediately inform them of my dispute with this debt.

Reporting information that you know to be inaccurate or failing to report information correctly violates the **Fair Credit Reporting Act § 1681s-2**. Should you pursue a judgment without validating this debt, I will inform the judge and request the case be dismissed based on your failure to comply with the FDCPA.

If you do NOT own the rights to collect this debt, I demand that you immediately send a copy of this dispute letter to the original creditor that you say I owe money, so they are also aware of my dispute with this debt.

Sincerely,

*Your Signature*

Your Name

This letter is to be sent after you have sent a debt validation letter and the collector **did not validate the debt within the 30-day time limit** or they didn't provide you with sufficient proof that the debt is yours.

Date:_____

Your Name
1234 Family Street
Hometown, MO 64118

To: ABC Collections Company
 1234 Harassment Street
 Collectors, N.Y. 10022

Re: Account #:_____

Hello ABC Collections Company,

I am writing in response to your {letter or phone call} dated {insert date of letter}, copy enclosed. On {insert date of initial dispute letter} I sent you a letter explaining that I do not believe I owe what you say I owe and, in accordance with the **Fair Debt Collection Practices Act 15 USC 1692g, Section 809(b) Validating Debts:**

**(b)** If the consumer notifies the debt collector in writing within the thirty-day period described in subsection **(a)** that the debt, or any portion thereof, is disputed, or that the consumer requests the name and address of the original creditor, the debt collector shall cease collection of the debt, or any disputed portion thereof, until the debt collector obtains verification of the debt or any copy of a judgment, or the name and address of the original creditor, and a copy of such verification or judgment, or name and address of the original creditor, is mailed to the consumer by the debt collector.

I must remind you that in my previous letter I requested the following information:

- (1) The amount of the debt;
- (2) The name of the creditor to whom the debt is owed
- (3) Provide a verification or copy of any judgment (if applicable)
- (4) Proof that you are licensed to collect debts in (insert your state)

I also requested that if you have reported me to any credit reporting agency, that you inform them that I have placed this debt in dispute and to provide me with proof that you have done so.

Furthermore, I asked that you immediately send a copy of that dispute letter to the company (creditor) that you say I owe money so they are also aware of my dispute with this debt.

As of today the 30-day, you have failed to respond to my request! For your convenience, I have included a copy of my previous letter and a copy of the mail receipt showing that you received my letter on {date}.

Since you have failed to respond I assume that you have been unable to validate the debt and therefore, I consider this matter closed. You may consider this letter your official notification that I do not intend to correspond with you on this matter again unless you comply with my requests, the FDCPA and the FCRA.

I must remind you that any attempt to collect this debt without validating it, violates the FDCPA and that I am recording all phone calls and keeping all correspondence concerning this matter.

Be advised that I will not hesitate to report violations of the law to my State Attorney General, the Federal Trade Commission and the national Better Business Bureau.

Sincerely,

*Your Signature*

Your Name

This letter is to be sent to the Credit Bureaus that fails to make changes, deletion or correct information in your credit file after sending them proof of the error. Make sure to select the correct Credit Bureau and address that you are sending the letter to by looking at the table below.

Date:_____

Your Name
1234 Family Street
Hometown, MO 64118

| Equifax | Experian | Trans Union |
|---|---|---|
| P.O. Box 740241 | P.O. Box 2014 | P.O. Box 1000 |
| Atlanta, GA 30374 | Allen, TX 75013 | Chester, PA 19022 |

Dear Equifax (Experian or Trans Union),

RE: Dispute Letter dated {date of initial letter}, and Follow-up Letter dated {date of second letter}

NOTICE OF INTENT TO FILE FORMAL FTC COMPLAINT:

This letter shall serve as formal notice of my intent to file a complaint with the Federal Trade Commission (FTC), due to your failure to respond to my two previous letters requesting a correction to my credit file.

As indicated by the enclosed copies of letters and mailing receipts, you have received from me by registered mail, a dispute letter dated {date of initial letter}, as well as a follow-up letter, dated {date of second letter}.

I am sure that you are aware of the Fair Credit Reporting Act's requirement to respond to consumer's credit report disputes within 30 days, and that the FTC investigates complaints for failure to respond. I have advised you on two separate occasions, more than 75 days ago and again 40 days ago that you are reporting inaccurate information about me. For the record and your benefit, I will restate my dispute:

- Line Item: {insert name of creditor, account number or line item number}
- Item Description: {this info is found on your credit report}
- Requested Correction: {describe exactly what you want: Deletion say so and explain why. Correction or Update, provide the correct information such as names, dates, etc. and any evidence to support your claim}

The Credit Ninja

The item above is completely {insert appropriate word: inaccurate, incorrect, incomplete, erroneous, misleading, outdated} and needs to be corrected immediately. I have enclosed a copy of your organization's credit report dated {insert date of report here} and for your convenience, circled the item(s) described above.

If you do not immediately take steps to resolve this issue, I will be forced to file a formal complaint with the FTC. Furthermore, I intend to consider seeking redress in civil court to recover damages, costs, and attorney fees, should you fail to respond.

Furthermore I expect you to supply me with a description of the procedure used to determine the accuracy and completeness of the disputed information, provide a corrected credit profile to me, all creditors who have received a copy within the last 6 months, and the last 2 years for employment purposes and the name, address, and telephone number of each credit grantor or other subscriber who have received a copy of my credit profile within the last 6 months.

If your re-investigation was negative, please supply the description of the procedure used to determine the accuracy and completeness of the information to my address above. If you have any questions concerning this matter I can be reached at {insert daytime phone number including area code}.

Sincerely,

*Your Signature*

Your Name

S.S.#_____

DOB:_____

*This letter gets sent when your only income is excluded from being garnished (SSI or SS check, disability, pension plans, annuity and retirement income). You can also send this letter if you don't have any property for a collector to attach a lien too, you need to send this before a collector takes you court.*

Date:_____

Your Name
1234 Family Street
Hometown, MO 64118

To: ABC Collections Company
    1234 Harassment Street
    Collectors, N.Y. 10022

                    Re: Account #:_____

Hello ABC Collections Company,

I am writing in response to your text message dated (Date Goes Here) about the above referenced account. I am unable to pay on this account due to the fact I'm on a limited "Social Security" Income of (amount goes here) per month. This is a permanent situation due to the fact I'm permanently disabled therefore I don't expect my income or situation to change anytime soon.

I also hope to save both of us a great deal of time, energy and expense by letting you know that I have no attachable income; essentially I have no money and can prove it! In accordance with the Fair Debt Collection Practices Act, 15 USC 1692c, 805(c):
(c) CEASING COMMUNICATION. **"If a consumer notifies a debt collector in writing that the consumer refuses to pay a debt** or that the consumer wishes the debt collector **to cease further communication with the consumer, the debt collector shall not communicate further with the consumer with respect to such debt..."**

Keep in mind that due to the fact I'm on permanent Social Security disability income that Social Security is a non-garnish able wage so therefore the chances of your company ever collecting on any judgment are extremely slim and therefore would cost your company more than its worth due to the fact that the chances of your company ever collecting on this debt are extremely low.

Although <u>I don't agree that I owe this debt</u>, I am unable to make any payments toward it and therefore ask that you cease further communication with me concerning this debt. I will notify you if my financial situation improves enough to allow me to begin making payments. Thank you.

Sincerely,

*Your Signature*

Your Name

Send this letter to all 3 credit bureaus if you don't want companies to pull your credit report to see if you're credit worthy enough to send you their credit card, or insurance offers. I hate that kind of mail so I send one to each credit bureau every year. I do this because the way I look at it if I want a credit card, credit line or insurance through a specific company I'll ask about it till then don't send my your junk type of mail. Make sure to select the correct Credit Bureau and address that you are sending the letter to by looking at the table below.

Date:_____

Your Name
1234 Family Street
Hometown, MO 64118

| Equifax | Experian | Trans Union |
|---|---|---|
| P.O. Box 740241 | P.O. Box 2014 | P.O. Box 1000 |
| Atlanta, GA 30374 | Allen, TX 75013 | Chester, PA 19022 |

Dear Equifax (Experian or Trans Union),

I request my name be removed from your marketing lists. Here is the information you require:

Your Name
1234 Family Street
Hometown, MO 64118

123 Panda Bear Lane
Beverly Hills, CA 90210

(Fill in your previous mailing address if you have moved in the last 6 months. If you have lived at this address for more than 6 months just put in your current address)

Thank you for your prompt handling of my request.

Sincerely,

*Your Signature*

Your Name
S.S.#_____
DOB:_____

This letter is to be sent when your sending a debt collector your final payment letting them know you have met your payment agreement and that you will no longer be sending them anymore payments. Keep record of all your payments.

Date:_____

Your Name
1234 Family Street
Hometown, MO 64118

To: ABC Collections Company
    1234 Harassment Street
    Collectors, N.Y. 10022

Re: Account #:_____

Hello ABC Collections Company,

My records show the balance on the above referenced account to be $_____. This letter is to inform you that in 30 days from the date of this letter I intend to send a final payment for that exact amount and mark it **"Paid in Full"**.

If you disagree with my calculations, I expect to receive a written explanation from you before 30 days. Otherwise I will assume you agree with my calculations and will accept my final payment and, after cashing my final payment my account should show as zero balance.

If you have any questions concerning this matter, I can be reached at {insert daytime phone number and area code}.

Sincerely,

*Your Signature*

Your Name

This letter is to be sent when your sending a debt collector your final payment letting them know you have met your payment agreement and that you will no longer be sending them anymore payments.

Date:_____

Your Name
1234 Family Street
Hometown, MO 64118

To: ABC Collections Company
    1234 Harassment Street
    Collectors, N.Y. 10022

Re: Account #:_____

Hello ABC Collections Company,

You'll find my final payment on the above referenced account enclosed. I request written confirmation showing this account as {paid in full or settled} according to our agreement on {insert date of agreement}.

However, should you choose not to provide me with confirmation, I will use your acceptance of this final payment as proof that you agree the account is {paid in full or settled}.

Now that this debt is paid, I do not expect to hear from you except to confirm the account is paid.

I will consider any other contact from you or you company as Harassment and will immediately report your actions to my State Attorney General and to the Federal Trade Commission and, if necessary, take whatever legal action is necessary to protect myself.

Finally, I expect you to remove this account and all references to my personal information from your records.

Sincerely,

*Your Signature*

Your Name

This letter is sent when you want to settle on a debt for the full amount but don't want to pay it in full upfront. Again always send a settlement contract with the letter. You can change the contract a little to meet any type of arrangement you are willing to agree to.

Date:_____

Your Name
1234 Family Street
Hometown, MO 64118

To: ABC Collections Company
    1234 Harassment Street
    Collectors, N.Y. 10022

    RE: Your {letter dated} or {phone call on date} reference account #: {place account or reference number here}

Hello ABC Collections Company,

According to my records and your {phone call or letter} the balance of this debt is $___.____. I am not disputing this debt however; my current financial situation prohibits me from paying the amount you're demanding. I am able to make payments on this account every {insert date of month} to your company in the amount of $_____.

I would appreciate a call or letter from you confirming your acceptance of my payment terms. However, if I do not hear from you, I will consider your action of cashing or depositing my check as confirmation that you accept my payment terms.

If you do not accept my terms then I expect the enclosed payment to be returned to me immediately in the enclosed self-addressed stamped envelope.

To show a good faith arrangement I've enclosed my first payment in the amount of $_____. If my financial situation improves enough for me to increase my payment amount I will contact you immediately. Thank you for understanding.

Sincerely,

*Your Signature*

Your Name

This letter is sent when you have made a payment arrangement and want to continue making payments but the debt collector refuses to take any smaller payments than what you previously agreed to. Keep a copy of the letter and send it <u>certified return receipt</u> so that way in the event you have to go to court over the debt you can show the judge that you were willing to make payments but the collector refused thus making it impossible for you to make any payment. When this happens most judges will rule in your favor and force the collector to take your payment for the lesser amount. It doesn't remove the debt but will allow you to make a smaller payment.

Date:_____

Your Name
1234 Family Street
Hometown, MO 64118

To: ABC Collections Company
    1234 Harassment Street
    Collectors, N.Y. 10022

Re: Account #:_____

Hello ABC Collections Company,

I have paid on this account per our payment agreement dated (insert date of verbal or written agreement). My records indicate that I have made (insert number) payments in the amount(s) of $(insert amount(s) for a total of $(insert total) in payments leaving a balance of $(insert balance).

Although I certainly want to continue paying on this debt, I simply cannot afford to pay the amount you are now demanding so, per your (phone call or letter) informing me that you refuse to accept my payments, you leave me no choice but to terminate our relationship.

For the record, do not contact me again regarding this account unless it is to inform me that my previous payment offer is acceptable or that you intend to take other actions as outlined in the **Fair Debt Collection Practice Act**.

Should you decide that some type of legal action is necessary, be advised that I welcome the opportunity to show any judge my efforts to resolve this issue. I have kept extremely accurate records of all correspondence and payments, and therefore, have complete confidence that any court would agree that my efforts have been in good faith.

Sincerely,

*Your Signature*

Your Name

This letter is sent when you have previously settled on a debt and have paid it in full but the debt collector is still trying to collect. You would also send this to any other collector who tries to collect on the debt and you would send proof of the debt being paid. Proof can be a cancelled check, money order payment stub, paid in full letter that was previously sent to you or any other method that shows the debt was paid.

Date:_____

Your Name
1234 Family Street
Hometown, MO 64118

To: ABC Collections Company
   1234 Harassment Street
   Collectors, N.Y. 10022

RE: Collection letter dated {date of letter here} or phone call on {date of call} reference account #: {account or reference number}

Hello ABC Collections Company,

This letter is to inform you that the account in question was settled (**or paid off**) on [insert date] with [insert name of collection agency].

I have enclosed copies of the settlement letter and proof of payment. You now have proof that this debt is no longer collectable, therefore I demand that you remove this account, and all references to my personal information, from your records.

I do not expect to hear from you again regarding this matter however, should you choose to ignore this notification, I will consider any contact not in accordance with the **Fair Debt Collection Act.**

This is a serious violation of the law and will immediately report any violations to my **State Attorney General** and to the **Federal Trade Commission** and, should it become necessary, take legal action to protect my myself.

Sincerely,
*Your Signature*
Your Name

This is the agreement you would send to the collector that you want them to sign when you both agree on a settlement. You can include this with any debt settlement offer that you send to the collector. You always want to have a collector sign one of these before you send them any payment because if a collector refuses to sign it then they won't honor any agreement you made and will more than likely start SOL again once you make a payment or worse they won't delete it from your credit reports. Never make a payment without a signed contract like this one.

Date:_____

Your Name
1234 Family Street
Hometown, MO 64118

To: ABC Collections Company
   1234 Harassment Street
   Collectors, N.Y. 10022

Re: Account #:_____

Sir or Madam,

On behalf of \_\_\_\_\_, hereafter referred to as Creditor and \_\_\_\_\_, hereafter referred to as "Debtor", agree to negotiate and settle the debt under the following terms and conditions.

The Creditor and Debtor agree that the current outstanding debt is $\_\_\_\_\_. Creditor agrees to accept less than the full amount of the debt provided that Debtor makes a payment for the agreed upon amount on {Date Goes Here}

Both parties agree that the Creditor will accept a cash payment of $\_\_\_\_\_ towards the settlement of the debt in full in order to receive a document by mail stating that the debt has been paid and is closed once the debtors payment clears.

Creditor also agrees to provide Debtor a letter stating that the debt is Paid As Agreed for the court upon receipt of agreed settlement amount of $\_\_\_\_\_.

This agreement for debt settlement shall be binding upon the Creditor, Debtor, and their successors and assignees.

Dated: _____
Signature: _____
Creditor: ABC Collection Company

Dated: _____
Signature: _____
Debtor: Your Name

This is the letter you would send to a collector when you want to settle a debt for pennies on the dollar. *Remember never settle for the full amount of the debt the collectors didn't purchase the debt for the full amount owed so why should you. However if it's the original creditor your chance is that you will have to pay the full amount, but once it's sold to a collector you have the right to settle for less. I usually start out with only 25% of the amount owed then I'll add another 5% more until I reach 50% I never settle for more. Remember the longer a debt collector has the debt the more likely they will settle for less rather than nothing at all if the debt reaches the SOL. Never send more than one settlement offer in a month. If they don't accept my first offer of 25% of the debt I wait another 3 to 4 months before sending another one of 30% and so on. I do this to make them hang onto the debt as the more likely they will want to settle. This method does work. You should always include the Settlement Contract in any offer you send so they can send it back confirming that they agree to your settlement offer.

Date:_____

Your Name
1234 Family Street
Hometown, MO 64118

To: ABC Collections Company
    1234 Harassment Street
    Collectors, N.Y. 10022

                      Re: Account #:_____

Hello ABC Collections Company,

This letter is in response to an entry on my credit report by your company ABC Harassment Company. I wish to save us both a lot of time and effort by settling this debt. Please be aware that this is not an acknowledgment or acceptance of the debt, as I have not received any validation or verification that this debt is even mine. Nor is this a promise to pay and is not a payment agreement unless you provide a response as detailed below.

I am aware that your company has the ability to report this debt to the credit bureaus, as you deem necessary. However I am aware that I have the right to proper validation of this debt, which means your company ABC Harassment Company would have to provide an accounting of this debt along with something from the original creditor proving that this debt is mine.

Further more I'm also aware that a creditor has the right to change a listing with the credit bureaus that they report. Which in this case the listing could be changed, removed or updated by your company ABC Harassment Company since your company is reporting the information to my credit reports.

I am willing to pay this debt in full in the amount of $_____ as a settlement for this debt. In return for your agreement to remove all information regarding this debt from all three of the credit reporting agencies or at the very least that ABC Harassment Company agrees to provide me with a faxed letter stating to me that the debt has been paid in full and should be removed from my credit reports.

The Credit Ninja

Upon receipt of a signed letter from ABC Harassment Company as described above I will pay this debt in full to ABC Harassment Company via _____ (your payment preference) payment in the amount of $_____.

If you agree and accept the terms please prepare a letter on your company letter head stating that you agree to remove the listing from all three of my credit reports or that your company agrees to provide me with a letter once payment is made in full stating that the debt is paid in full and should be removed from my credit reports.

Please forward your agreement to me via the United States Post Office so that I can get a prompt payment to your company for the full amount of $_____.

Sincerely,

*Your Signature*

Your Name

This letter is sent when a company pulls your credit without your permission, which results as an inquiry on your credit reports and lowers your score.

Date:_____

Your Name
1234 Family Street
Hometown, MO 64118

To: ABC Collections Company
  1234 Harassment Street
  Collectors, N.Y. 10022

RE: Unauthorized Credit Pull

To whom it may concern:

As per my Equifax credit report, your company obtained my credit file on (date here).

I do not recall applying for credit or employment with ABC Harassment Company. Per the FCRA § 616. Civil liability for willful noncompliance [15 U.S.C. § 1681n]

"(b) Civil liability for knowing noncompliance. Any person who obtains a consumer report from a consumer reporting agency under false pretenses or knowingly without a permissible purpose shall be liable to the consumer reporting agency for actual damages sustained by the consumer reporting agency or $1,000, whichever is greater."

From the FTC opinion letter Mr. Greenblatt, which states the following:

"Any person who procures a consumer report under false pretenses, or knowingly without a permissible purpose, is liable for $1000 or actual damages (whichever is greater) to both the consumer and to the consumer reporting agency from which the report is procured."

Please explain your permissible purpose for your obtaining my credit file. Should you not have a permissible purpose, please arrange for payment of $1,000 by __/___/__ (which should be 30 days from the date of when you mail the letter). Please respond via postal mail.

Sincerely,

*Your Signature*

Your Name

This letter is sent after you send a dispute to one of the credit bureaus and they send you a letter stating that the debt was validated and you still think that the debt is invalid and shouldn't be on your credit report. Sometimes a credit bureau will use automated validation methods that are not accurate so it's always good to find out how the debt was validated and this letter will do that.                Date:_____

Your Name
1234 Family Street
Hometown, MO 64118

| Equifax | Experian | Trans Union |
|---|---|---|
| P.O. Box 740241 | P.O. Box 2014 | P.O. Box 1000 |
| Atlanta, GA 30374 | Allen, TX 75013 | Chester, PA 19022 |

Hello Equifax (Experian or Trans Union),

I have sent many letters your company regarding the errors which I have. But they continue to remain in my consumer credit report. I am again noting that problems have been discovered and they continue to remain unresolved. I urge Equifax to remove the following accounts, as they are not mine.

ABC Collections Company
1234 Harassment Street
Collectors, N.Y. 10022

Since you have not given me names of persons with their business addresses that you contacted for re-verification of the information, so that I could follow up as I requested. I assume that you have not been able to verify the information I have disputed.
If this problem continues and I am forced to seek some form of professional assistance. Therefore you have been forewarned of the harm which this problem is causing me. I am hereby giving you 30 days from the date of receipt of this letter unless you provide me with a verifiable excuse why this account can't be verified in a timely fashion.

Please send me an updated copy of my credit report providing me proof that this account has been deleted from my credit file. I look forward to a timely response from your company.

Sincerely,

*Your Signature*

Your Name
S.S.#_____
DOB:_____

*This letter is sent after you send a dispute to one of the credit bureaus and they send you a letter stating that the debt was validated and you still think that the debt is invalid and shouldn't be on your credit report. Sometimes a credit bureau will use automated validation methods that are not accurate so it's always good to find out how the debt was validated and this letter will do that.*

Date:_____

Your Name
1234 Family Street
Hometown, MO 64118

| Equifax | Experian | Trans Union |
|---|---|---|
| P.O. Box 740241 | P.O. Box 2014 | P.O. Box 1000 |
| Atlanta, GA 30374 | Allen, TX 75013 | Chester, PA 19022 |

Hello Equifax (Experian or Trans Union),

I have just received my credit report and have noted that it contains erroneous information regarding the following accounts. I would like them deleted from my report. I am requesting that you delete the following account from all three of my credit files, as they do not reflect my actual credit worthiness.

ABC Collection Company,
Account# _____

When I questioned ABC Collection Company about this account, they told me they requested this account to be removed from my credit report. Per applicable laws I am requesting that you provide me with the method your company used to verify this debt?

Please note that your validation method must be done using a method that does not violate my **Constitutional Rights**.

Please notify me if it takes longer. Please send names and business addresses of those persons you contacted for any verification Also, as per the **Fair Credit Reporting Act**. Please send me an updated copy of my credit report showing that this account has been deleted from my credit file or the validation method is not violating my **Civil & Constitutional Rights**.

Sincerely,

*Your Signature*

Your Name

S.S.#_____

DOB:_____

This letter is sent after you send a dispute to one of the credit bureaus and they send you a letter stating that the debt was validated and you still think that the debt is invalid and shouldn't be on your credit report. Sometimes a credit bureau will use automated validation methods that are not accurate so it's always good to find out how the debt was validated and this letter will do that.

Date:_____

Your Name
1234 Family Street
Hometown, MO 64118

To: ABC Collections Company
    1234 Harassment Street
    Collectors, N.Y. 10022

                Re: Account #:_____

Hello ABC Collections Company,

This letter is to inform you that I still dispute this debt. After receiving your response to my original dispute letter, I contacted the original creditor who was unable to verify this account as mine.

In my opinion, you have failed to validate this debt. I must remind you that I originally disputed this debt within the 30-day dispute period outlined in the FDCPA and that I am now also responding in a timely manner to your attempt to validate this debt.

Because I still consider this debt, as "still in dispute" I do not expect to hear from you again except to provide information or documentation to clear up my reasons for disputing this debt.

I already advised you in my previous letter that I am fully aware of my rights under the **Fair Debt Collection Practices Act** and the **Fair Credit Reporting Act** and that I will not hesitate to take all legal steps necessary to protect myself.
Be advised that I am keeping accurate records of all correspondence including tape recording all phone calls.

Sincerely,
*Your Signature*
Your Name

# Conclusion

Now that you know about all the different parts of your credit report; how your credit score is determined and how to dispute and validate information on your credit. You should have no problems fixing your score and disputing information on your credit report. Just remember that there is no easy fix to repairing your credit as it does take time and patients regardless of whether you go about doing it yourself or utilizing the services of a credit repair agency.

All of the information along with all of the bonuses to this book should make your journey to better credit an easier journey now that you know all about your credit and how to go about repairing your credit.

Once again, we are not attorneys nor we aren't licensed attorneys in any State of the United States of North America. Any of the information here is not intended to be legal advice; the information contained in this book is for informational purposes only. If you need legal advice regarding your credit you should obtain legal advice from a licensed attorney. The information in this book doesn't guarantee that you will increase your credit score as your score is based on many different factors and laws. This book is written with the sole intention of personal use and strictly educational it is not a guarantee of any results

## ABOUT THE BOOK

This Book is written to help educate people about their credit, credit scores and the laws that shape how your credit scores will affect your everyday life. It is no secret that our credit scores control our lives. Credit scores can determine what kind of house we can purchase, what car we can drive, the car insurance rates, the interest on our credit cards and even potential employers...

This book will help you understand your Credit Reports, Credit Scores and Credit Laws that everyone should know but they do not want you to know. In addition you will find very useful tools to help you claim your credit rating back and defend yourself from ABUSIVE collection agents and their companies.

www.ingramcontent.com/pod-product-compliance
Lightning Source LLC
Chambersburg PA
CBHW051810170526
45167CB00005B/1958